INDUSTRIAL CHIC

INDUSTRIAL CHIC
CULT FURNITURE, DESIGN AND LIGHTING

BRIGITTE DURIEUX & LAZIZ HAMANI

WITH THE COLLABORATION OF ELODIE PALASSE-LEROUX

WITH OVER 250 COLOUR ILLUSTRATIONS

Thames & Hudson

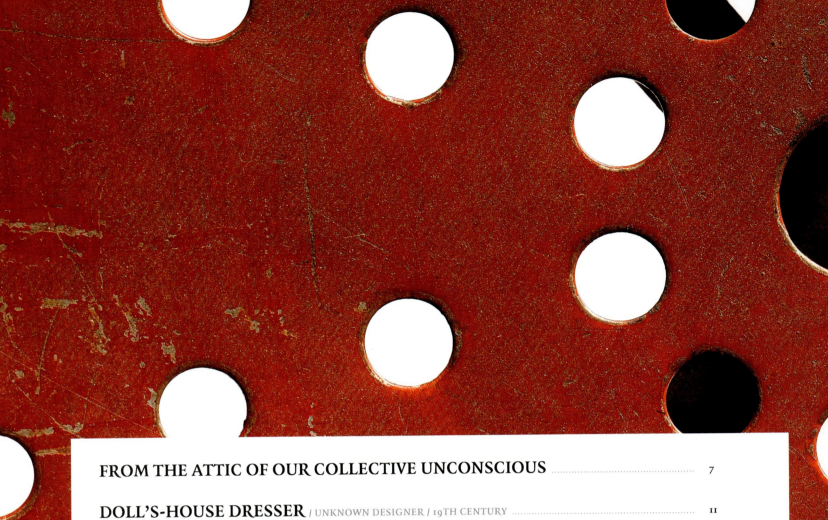

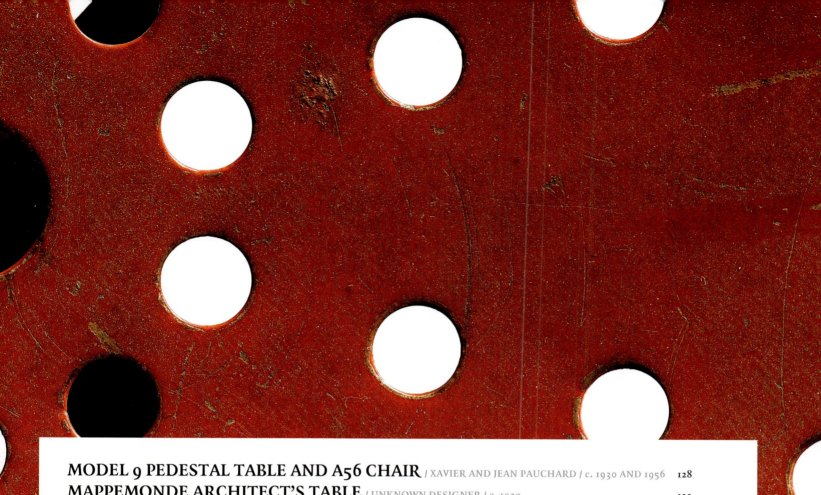

FROM THE ATTIC OF OUR COLLECTIVE UNCONSCIOUS

FRENCH METAL

Paris, 1995. In Gilles Oudin's shop window display on the rue du Bouloi stood a Scherf bookcase, two pieces of post-room furniture and some Gras lamps. 'People used to come in and ask me what I was selling. I would tell them I owned a garage!'

But thanks to a clientele drawn predominantly from artistic circles, this pioneering industrial antiques shop in Paris prospered, and so did its unusual selection of furniture. Oudin also began to hold exhibitions and spread the word about

industrial design through the media, which endlessly fascinated this erudite little man, a connoisseur in terms of both his natural curiosity and his knowledge of classic styles. 'All those chests of drawers, chairs and desks were getting incredibly boring. And then I just couldn't afford it any more.' And now the man who hated all those 'Louis Is, Louis IIs and Louis IIIs' has become the king of his own industrial realm.

A few years later, at the other end of France, Bernard Mouiren also became a convert to the cause of industrial design. On the advice of a scrap-metal dealer, he claims he 'bought it because I liked it, but it didn't sell!' But Mouiren is a specialist, and had been working with sheet metal for years in his native Provence. A car mechanic who married a dealer's daughter and took over the store, he used to believe that the antiques trade primarily involved traditional furniture, trinkets and ceramics. Was he bored? Of course he was. But one day in 2000, 'I came face to face with a metal shelving unit, right in the middle of all the Louis-Philippe and Henri II furniture, and I bought it.'

Not far away in the village of Isle-sur-la-Sorgue, Laurent Ardonceau also succumbed to the same passion. Soon, not even the smallest scrap of metal could escape his quest for industrial bargains. 'It's a feeling as well as a kind of poetry,' he says of the youthful intuition that has now made this Beaux-Arts graduate into a star of the industrial design landscape. A few years ago he was picking up Jieldé lamps and Tolix chairs for peanuts: 'I couldn't sell them, so I stockpiled them. I sold the first heavy industrial objects, work tables and strong boxes, to Bernard; he was the only person mad enough to take all this strange scrap metal off our hands. He was the only one who got it.'

Meanwhile, Jérôme Lepert was rummaging around on the Grésillons industrial estate in Gennevilliers. Overalls donned over a suit and tie, this former company president is now the chief of industrial style, finding a rich harvest of objects in former ironworks and paint factories in the Paris suburbs. He has never stopped rummaging in this way. It has even become his trademark – striding up and down a factory floor in search of a lamp or tracking down an original Nicolle stool, an item that he now manufactures himself.

These people are the pioneers of industrial chic in France, setting a style and inspiring others with the passion to follow it too. They have breathed new life into a world once condemned to the scrap heap, rediscovering its secrets and making it glorious again. Thanks to their efforts, the classics of French industrial design are now sought after and exported all over the world.

UPCYCLING USA

New York, 1995. In a store in the heart of Tribeca, office furniture and wooden and metal seats, tables and bank counters filled the shop window. The industrial revolution had conquered Europe and was now making its way in the United States. Just as they were once pioneers of the industrial drive for progress, New Yorkers were now rediscovering a style of furniture that had been left out in the cold by the city's first loft-dwellers, who had chosen to ignore it in the 1970s and instead preferred to fill their high-ceilinged, metal-beamed homes with bric-a-brac, folk art or furniture from the 1950s.

Not far away, the same trend was on full view at the showrooms of Urban Archaeology. The best of the new 'salvage' trend was on show there, including original Holophane lights, drawing tables, old bathroom taps and spiral staircases. 'This work inspired me a lot,' Jérôme Lepert remembers today; in fact, he was so captivated by the concept that his business card now describes him as an 'industrial archaeologist'.

The industrial history of North America had produced huge quantities of objects, and as in Europe, there was a sense of nostalgia in the design community for this form of design and its approach to materials, a feeling that quickly spread to the general public.

The changing status of the Tolix Model A chair among dealers over the last couple of decades is an example. 'Between 1988 and 1989,' recalls international buyer Annick Ricochon, 'when Paul Hawken was the first to include galvanized steel Tolix chairs in his mail-order catalogue, he was probably thinking about the authenticity and unusual nature of these pieces, but he could sell them to his clients by focusing on the fact that the chairs are rustproof, and therefore solid and durable. But in terms of promoting the industrial aesthetic, it was the Sundance Catalog that featured Xavier Pauchard's chair in 1995 and pushed it to huge success: now some six thousand Tolix chairs are sold in the US every year.'

A GLOBAL MELTING POT

Industrial design, like everything else in life, now criss-crosses the world. As a French brand name is becoming a must-have item among US shoppers, American dealers can be found scouring the second-hand markets of France, looking for undiscovered classics. Between 2000 and 2004, the clichés of 'French' interior style in the United States – painted furniture, red-checked tablecloths, charming basketwork – were almost erased by the dominance of French industrial design. Industrial furniture was exported by the truckload: tables, shelving units and workbenches in huge numbers, along with the best products of French ironworks of the late 19th and early 20th centuries, with anything recalling classic design shapes and the spirit of Gustave Eiffel being particularly successful.

This new economy very quickly set its own standards. Whereas Europeans admired the original patinas of blue, green, red and orange, Francine Gardner began designing industrial-style interiors for the American brand Intérieurs in 1994 and favoured traditional, unadorned metal for her heavy cabinets, cast-iron tables and tool benches.

THE RISK OF OVERKILL

The trend we are now witnessing is a love of industrial design in its purest and simplest form. Singer sewing machines cover the walls of the stores of the All Saints chain, ship's strongboxes are found at L'Éclaireur in Paris, and foundry furniture is embraced by the Dutch designer Piet Hein Eek in Eindhoven. And it can also be eclectic and elegantly upcycled, as seen at the most stylish boutiques of New York and Paris.

Industrial style is constantly being revived and reinvented. 'Decorative trends,' says Vincent Grégoire from the Nelly Rodi design studio, 'are rooted more strongly in the cultures of northern Europe, the cultures that remind us of the industrial past, that deal with heavy metals and construction.'

'But be careful,' warns Daniel Rozenstroch, 'copies from China and India are now becoming more widespread, making this style of furniture more commonplace.' The creative director of lifestyle magazine *Marie-Claire Maison*, himself a great collector of industrial furniture, is firm in his belief that cheap mass-produced imports could eventually diminish the status of industrial style.

Will industrial furniture become a victim of its own success? Not while the story of these objects unearthed from our collective unconscious is still being told.

Brigitte Durieux

This item of miniature furniture, a rare toy for a little girl, was found in the Saint-Étienne region. Made from stamped metal, it has wrought-iron balustered feet and handles attached with a hammer, and riveted hinges.

DOLL'S-HOUSE DRESSER

UNKNOWN DESIGNER | 19TH CENTURY

The practice of factory workers making small items for their own personal use using company materials and equipment has existed for a long time. Such items are often known as side productions or 'homers'.

Although frequently tolerated, the misappropriation of scraps was generally against regulations. Creating these items from raw materials was a mild form of fraud, and required the silent collusion of skilled workers with their immediate superiors.[1] 'In the evening they would take out of their bag empty bottles, their dirty lunchbox, a newspaper, and sometimes scraps of metal "that might come in useful", trying to create items out of wrought iron, or everyday objects with whatever came to hand.'[2]

These 'homers' were the result of hard work, of course, but not that imposed by the company, rather, work that they carried out for themselves. This practice was something of a safeguard, reintroducing as it did a personal touch that had been wiped out in a world in which work was graded, sanitized and regulated down to the very last detail.[3]

These small objects also reveal the skill of the workers, their mastery of the trivial. The details of this piece of doll's-house furniture are also evidence of the thoroughness paid to the manufacturing process. The tiny hinged doors and drawer handles show the same sophisticated techniques of stamping, riveting, bending and turning of the metal used in full-sized furniture.

As well as displaying its maker's mastery of different skills, every 'homer' tells a story of humanity, rebellion, complicity and regulations, and – through its form – of the evolution of style. Each is at the same time a witness to a different period and a fragment of social and cultural history.

1 Bernard Clément explains this in a note on the practice in *Les Schneider, Le Creusot: A family, a company, a city: 1836–1960*, Musée d'Orsay, Paris, 1995.
2 Martine Sonnet in *Atelier 62*.
3 *Les Schneider, Le Creusot: A family, a company, a city: 1836–1960*, Musée d'Orsay, Paris, 1995.

FACTORY LOCKER

GANTOIS / 19TH CENTURY

The 'health and safety' laws of 1893 and 1903 made their presence felt in France. The rattling of the padlock that secured the locker door accompanied the transition from private life to the professional sphere, and vice versa. Internal compartments (soiled clothing had to be kept separate), hangers and hooks housed the workers' personal and professional items; they shed their skin every morning and evening.

At first made from wood, then from metal (initially with grated fronts that later became solid), lockers can be seen as the first 'social' piece of furniture. Modern lockers do not hold the same secrets as those of the past: 'odds and ends' made in secret during working hours, mattresses for sleeping on, small souvenirs and treasured personal items, trade union leaflets and even children that could not be looked after elsewhere. These lockers were a private space in the workplace, a sacred enclave in a communal world. Thanks only to the presence of the padlock, they resisted the suspicion of an employer as well as the curiosity or greed of colleagues.

Under strict surveillance, lockers also became a symbol of social struggle; those punched with a number or sporting a label allowed supervisors to quickly identify any workers who returned outside permitted hours: 'representatives at ironworks demanded one locker per person... They were well aware that the labelling was intended to facilitate the work of the supervisor during her rounds, when she might catch someone who should not have been there. Because whatever the blacksmiths aspired to, it was to be left in peace at their lockers.'[1] They were a place of confrontation between workers and employers. At Renault, in the early 1930s, the staff manager announced his intention to Louis Renault to 'replace all the locker supervisors.

I need smart men to search the lockers and find any communist propaganda material lying around in the pockets of the staff.'[2]

A place where private life met hard work, lockers played a full part in the story of the lives of workers, so much so that they gave rise to a number of expressions, many of which are still in use: a worker fired from the factory was asked to 'take his locker', while striking workers proclaimed their displeasure by 'returning to the lockers'.

Two manufacturing processes indicate the creator of this locker (J. Gantois & Beucher Furniture Makers in Saint-Dié-des-Vosges): the punctured sheet metal (still one of the specialities of this company), and the upper cornice made from rolled sheet metal fitted with a wooden tube.

1 Martine Sonnet, *Atelier 62*.
2 Saint Loup, Renault de Billancourt.

Originally wall-mounted, this unit is 195 cm (76¾ in.) long, 25 cm (9⅞ in.) high and 40 cm (15¾ in.) deep. Its five lockers would have had coat hooks fixed underneath.

STRONGBOX

It all began in England, with an impregnable lock. In 1784 Joseph Bramah patented a mechanism that was impossible to force, and founded the Bramah Locks Company. An American locksmith, Alfred C. Hobbs, succeeded in opening it and in turn began to manufacture strongboxes. As for the armour plating, this we owe in large part to two British brothers, Charles and Jeremiah Chubb, who invented it in 1835. Ten years earlier, in France, a certain Alexandre Fichet had opened a locksmith shop in Paris.

Having been restored, this heavy piece of furniture (weighing approximately 100 kg, or 220 lb) still fulfils its function and fits in perfectly with the 'industrial' trend. The fact that ship's strongboxes have become particularly sought-after items is probably owed to their striking designs, with their iron cladding, wrought-iron keys and long nails and their invisible locking mechanism, along with customized decorative motifs in brass (strongboxes containing pharmaceutical items, for example, sported a caduceus).

With a shape that is often encountered in the plots dreamed up by Arthur Conan Doyle and in other fictional tales from the 19th century, the strongbox is perhaps the most iconic piece of furniture of the Industrial Revolution. During this period of fierce economic competition, it soon became indispensable, holding as it did the cash, patents and valuable papers that guaranteed a company's survival. The fact that it was fireproof, one of the major selling points of industrial furniture, also served to increase its sales.

The first ship's strongboxes were made from wood. This oak crate, measuring 88 cm (34⅝ in.) high, 60.5 cm (23¾ in.) wide, and 38.5 cm (15 in.) deep, has been assembled using a traditional dovetail system and is decorated with braided straps held in place by long wrought-iron nails, sometimes 5 cm (2½ in.) in length. The design pictured here weighs 180 kg (397 lb).

VOLTAIRE CHAIR

GRASSIN-BALEDANS / LATE 19TH CENTURY

Just as comfortable and stylish as their counterparts made for the refined atmosphere of the salons, these pieces of furniture were designed for outdoor use. The generic name of 'Arras furniture' is now applied to garden furniture produced by industrial manufacturers in the Arras region of France between 1840 and 1920 from a material known as *fer élégi*.[1] Heirs to the founders of the Industrial Revolution,[2] these were the masters of a new way of living – the privileged classes who were discovering the pleasures and virtues of life in the open air.

Using their ingenuity, they competed to devise new techniques, producing glasshouses, verandas, cages, aviaries and even ready-to-use stables. They provided towns with covered markets, huge structures and bandstands; they installed railings and gates in the squares and gardens that Baron Haussmann was creating by the hundred.

It was in the midst of this Second Empire euphoria that the artistic ironwork manufacturer Grassin-Baledans[3] opened its doors in Saint-Sauveur-lez-Arras in 1864. It specialized in the manufacture of solid and extruded iron for parks and gardens. Léonce Eugène Grassin-Baledans, the founder, who had spent a long time as an ordinary worker, soon employed several hundred salaried employees. A visionary, he guessed that wrought iron would be the future, and filed the first patent for a semicircular hollow form of metal, with which he created numerous objects.

One particular example bears witness to its success: on 15 September 1874, following his election to office, Maréchal de Mac-Mahon (1808–93), President of the Republic of France, came in person to visit the factory belonging to 'this great French industrialist'.

The pages of the Grassin-Baledans catalogue, 'supplier to the State and the principal cities of France, including Paris', included gates, items for the farm, garden or stable, glasshouses, verandas, bridges, walkways, kiosks and staircases, as well as twenty pieces of garden furniture. Plant pots, tables, chairs, benches, stools and footrests are recognizable by their lion's-paw or horse's-hoof feet, in fact an extremely practical novelty as this broad base prevented the furniture from sinking into the soil.

The refined and robust – not to mention expensive – manufacturing of this furniture intended it for high-end clientele, both in France itself and abroad. Pieces in the Napoleon III, Art Nouveau and Art Deco styles won prizes at the universal exhibitions in Paris, London and Brussels. They were exported to Great Britain and the United States, and even to Australia and Asia.

1 This term refers to a semi-hollow, oblong-shaped extruded steel tubing.
2 Such as Carré (Paris), Guillot Pelletier and Jouffray (Orléans) and Blod-Galland (Tournus).
3 Located near the front line, the company struggled to market a style of furniture that was considered old-fashioned after the two world wars, and began to concentrate on metal for the building trade. Taken over by Éric Bouët (president of France's metal construction union from 1979 to 1983) in the 1970s, it won a contract for building cinemas for the Iraqi army. Conflict put an end to the contract and to this hundred-year-old firm.

The design pictured here is a detail of the so-called 'Dutch' chair, no. 17, Voltaire model, measuring 103 cm (40½ in.) high and 68 cm (26¾ in.) wide, with a seat height of 37 cm (14⅝ in.). A version with a swivel base was also produced. Original catalogue price: painted wicker 27 francs; painted white 29 francs.

Arras furniture is now very popular with antiques hunters thanks to its 'fin de siècle' appeal. The lion's-paw feet are typical of those produced by Grassin-Baledans in the 1850s. The horse's-hoof foot was adopted by the Saint-Sauveur manufacturers in the early 20th century.

IDEAL
BOOKCASE

THÉODORE SCHERF / C. 1880

Théodore Scherf's grandson is still surprised by its success even today.[1] 'The rack system already existed, but only in wood. My grandfather simply came up with the idea of fitting bookcases with a metal rack.' A crucial detail that hastened the destiny of this 'manufacturer of iron rails'.[2]

    With metal architecture in the spirit of Eiffel, solid wooden shelves and flat-arched iron struts with crossover

[1] The Scherf bookcase won awards at the Salons in Brussels (1888) and Paris (Scherf was the recipient of a silver medal in 1885, 1894, 1895, 1896 and 1900, and a bronze medal in 1889).

[2] Listed in the *Annuaire de l'Association des inventeurs et artistes industriels (France)* in 1889 as 'SCHERF, manufacturer of iron rails, 36 rue des Acacias, Paris'.

reinforcements, Scherf's bookcase was symbolic of the emergence of the service sector. As well as to retailers (for shopfitting) it was predominantly provided to 'suppliers to institutes, to public healthcare, to the Paris Chamber of Commerce, to goverment ministries, railway companies . . . and numerous public libraries across France, its colonies and overseas'.

Some private individuals allowed themselves to be captivated by these 'open' pieces of furniture. Those with a keen eye for hygiene denounced traditional glass-fronted bookcases, accusing them of encouraging the growth of mould and insects thanks to the lack of circulating air.

In 1896, the weekly magazine *La Science Illustrée* sang its praises, considering it perfectly suited to 'the increasingly small size of modern apartments'. The last cholera epidemic had only just come to an end and the use of metal was strongly encouraged. 'Until now', the journalist continued, 'iron has only made a timid appearance in furniture, being used almost exclusively for sleeping berths, but if used intelligently, it deserves to be employed on a wider scale.'

After the death of its founder in 1907, Scherf's firm continued to prosper under the joint leadership of his widow and son-in-law, followed by that of his son Théodore Scherf. Philippe Scherf went on to keep the family business going until 1980, manufacturing metal storage shelves.

Cornice, steel column uprights with capitals, polished bands and oak shelves: this Scherf bookcase is 1.2 m (47¼ in.) high by 90 cm (35⅜ in.) wide and is signed with a brass plaque bearing the inscription 'TH. SCHERF 35 rue d'Aboukir Paris'. This is an unusually luxurious model, with striking Art Nouveau-style arches.

A prismatic lamp with a cast-aluminium shade: this Holophane design was produced between the 1930s and the 1950s. The glass lamp has a circumference of 33 cm (13 in.) and an overall height of 40 cm (15¾ in.).

DIFFUSER-SHADE LIGHT

HOLOPHANE / 1893

The story of this system of 'industrial' lighting, designed more than a century ago, is also the story of the Holophane Company.

In the late 19th century, daylight and gas lamps were no longer sufficient to provide light for workers in factories and workshops in the early morning and at dusk. The advent of electricity soon saw the hanging of metal plates fixed to ceilings and walls, but they fulfilled their function too well and dazzled the workers.

It was Frenchman Antoine Blondel who first came up with the idea for prismatic glass in 1893. A professor of electricity at the French National School of Bridges and Roads, Blondel patented a new round lamp which he called a 'Holophane', from the Greek words *holos*, 'whole', and *phanos*, 'light'. The different sides of his transparent glass lamp 'harnessed' and channelled the light much more efficiently.

The rights to the patent were purchased by the American Otis A. Mygatt in 1896. The company

Holophane Ltd was formed in Great Britain (for a time, the term 'holophane' was used generically to describe any diffuser lamp), while the United States was home to Holophane Inc. The French branch, the Société Anonyme Holophane, was founded in 1920.

The prismatic glass was suitable for all types of mounts, allowing the system to be adapted for all possible uses: both indoors and outdoors, for display-case spotlights, lamps, chandeliers and street lighting. Holophane soon equipped factories and workshops, warehouses and gymnasiums, exhibition halls and entertainment venues, stations and schools.

The Second World War slowed the growth of the firm, and its various branches met with different fates. Holophane France is now the world's leading supplier of car headlamp glass, while Holophane US is proud of its position as the world's leading lighting supplier.

BRILLIÉ CLOCK

BRILLIÉ FRÈRES WORKSHOP / 1900

A monumental clock on the factory façade, pitiless timekeeper with its impetuous chimes: the age of streamlining and the regulation of tasks had sounded. Discipline and punctuality were no longer enough. The theories of the American engineer Frederick Winslow Taylor (1856–1915) had been widely picked up on; time was now counted and time regulated industry. The rhythm of the clock dictated the rhythm of actions repeated throughout the day with mechanical regularity. 'The machines cost money, they had to run. Their movement was regular; work had to be as well.'[1]

In 1898, Charles Vigreux and Lucien Brillié formed a company manufacturing 'mechanical and electrical equipment' in Levallois-Perret. The latter, assisted by his brother Henri, wasted no time in developing specific expertise; the workshop of Brillié Frères adapted its clocks to run on electricity, making them infallible and impregnable. Countless factories, stations and schools in France and abroad adopted them. In a catalogue dating from the 1920s, the Brillié Frères' workshop listed the designs on which its reputation was founded: 'free-standing clocks, timekeeping systems, automatic calls and rings, staff entry recorders, building clocks, bells and chimes, synchronization of all timekeeping equipment, alarm clocks, rounds monitor, and chronographs.'

1 Alain Dewerpe, *Histoire du travail*, Paris, 2001.

Industry was regulated by streamlined and timed production. Thanks to Lucien Brillié's invention, the reliability of a clock was no longer reliant on the person responsible for winding it, but on electricity.

RAVEL REVOLVING POSTCARD RACK

LOUIS-DIDIER DES GACHONS / C. 1900

A new generation of inventors rose to prominence at the start of the 20th century. They had wide-ranging interests and refused to be limited to a single field. Having now been mastered, metal could be bent to the will of inventors and became the preferred material of manufacturers keen on innovation.

Louis-Didier des Gachons (1875–1951) belonged to this generation. A publisher of postcards, director of a magazine and inventor of a coloured lithograph process, he accumulated many patents: drawing pins and paper clips, bookends and filing cabinets, and in particular, a revolving postcard rack, the *Classeur sans fin* (Endless Cabinet), introduced in 1900 at the Universal Exhibition. This invention marked a real turning point in his life; abandoning photogravure to devote himself to his patents, in 1905 he formed a company with the self-explanatory name of 'The Revolving Rack and Cabinet Manufacturer' (Industrie du Tourniquet et du Classeur). In 1922 he also began to produce the Gras lamp.

With its half-metal, half-wooden casing, its continuous winder and a hundred postcards, this display unit was manufactured by the thousand between 1905 and 1970, first by the Industrie du Tourniquet et du Classeur, then from 1929 by the Ravel Company.[1] Given as a gift by postcard publishers to their customers, it was soon set up in tobacconists and station kiosks. Bookshops preferred its smaller twin, a floor rack that stood on four wooden legs.

1 In June 1927, Didier des Gachons went into partnership with one of his associates, André René Ravel, forming the company Didier des Gachons and Ravel. See Didier Teissonnière, *La Lampe Gras*, Paris, 2008.

This rare example dates from the 1950s, as demonstrated by its black-painted chest, the size of the postcards – 9 cm (3½ in.) by 14 cm (5½ in.) – and the bolted-on tricolour label reading 'Les spécialités RAVEL, constructeurs à Clamart'.

HANDLING AND STORAGE BOXES

SUROY FRÈRES / 1902

Unearthed in antiques shops, factory boxes are now making their way into people's homes. But before this new lease of life, they were part of the social history of the 19th and 20th centuries. Still echoing with the ticking of the workshop clock, their story is that of company logistics and the dizzying race to increase efficiency and production.

Metal boxes were first introduced during the Industrial Revolution, replacing wicker baskets and wooden containers. Industries quickly kitted out their workshops with metal equipment in place of wood. Raw materials, packed into boxes by the workers' feet, were transformed by machines into finished products that would find their way into a second box, the final stage of this routine labour.

Storage boxes and silver cans made by Suroy Frères, with their beautiful patina, evoke both the history of the company and working conditions since the Industrial Revolution.

The first manufacturer of metal boxes was the Penn Metal Corporation, founded in Pennsylvania in 1869; its boxes accompanied the boom in industry across the United States. Europe followed at the turn of the century. In France, in 1902, the Suroy brothers began to specialize in boxes and 'silver cans' for the textile industry.[1] Rectangular or cylindrical and available in many sizes, the boxes were made from pressed cardboard, varnished a deep brownish red, riveted and fitted with steel reinforcements and rigid handles.

Some years later, the drive for industrial efficiency promoted by Frederick Taylor Winslow began to create new pressures in the working environment. The pace was stepped up and the performance of workers was measured by the boxes that held the fruits of their labour: the quantity of products made in a given time could be gauged, thus allowing salaries to be fixed. The boxes themselves therefore became the focus of anxiety: 'In the evening I once again lose time looking for a box, and then, after failing to find one, decanting pieces into a basket taken from the next machine. And the box into which almost 16,000 pieces have dropped is so heavy to handle that I have to empty it into another,' recorded Simone Weil in 1936 in *La Condition ouvrière*.

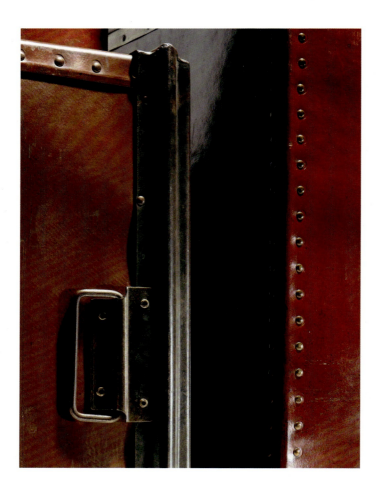

1 As well as handling materials for the textile industry and trolleys for collecting cloth or waste, the company, based in Loos in northern France, also developed textiles for hospital use and rubber containers for the automotive industry. Despite a diversification policy over the long term, Suroy closed in 2004 amid the severe crisis affecting the textile industry.

GALVANIZED-STEEL BUCKET

ÉTABLISSEMENTS X. PAUCHARD / 1907

Jugs, coal scuttles, pots, pans, clothes boilers, tubs, waste bins, watering cans, feeding and water troughs, weathervanes, railings and stakes: from the late 19th century the invention of sheet steel and galvanization gave rise to a whole range of items for cooking, cleaning, the home, the garden, looking after livestock and agricultural production.

It was several decades before this process, which had been invented on the other side of the Atlantic, was industrialized in France. A young zinc worker from France's Morvan region, Xavier Pauchard, the son and grandson of an itinerant roofer and zinc worker, developed an interest in 1907. In order to perfect his knowledge and to develop new uses, he ordered a generously illustrated book on the subject from the United States. Setting up on an abandoned plot of land far from prying eyes, Xavier Pauchard carried out experiments in the bottom of old pots. Neither the harsh climate nor successive failures, nor even the onset of poisoning, could stop him: he went on to master galvanized steel. Whether used for everyday items or for outdoor furniture, galvanization owes its pedigree to Pouchard's tenacity.

A page had turned: galvanization opened up new horizons for working with steel. Sheet metal manufacturers soon took over from artisanal metal workers. Zinc never ceased to be reborn; and so, in a somewhat paradoxical fashion, this 'rustproof' metal saw Tolix chairs move from the garden into the home in the 1990s. Its attractive metal appearance, originally conceived to provide protection against rust, created a new aesthetic. Industrial style had found its signature.

Measuring 31 cm (12¼ in.) in diameter, 35 cm (13¾ in.) high, having 56 rivets, weighing 4.6 kg (10.2 lb) when empty, up to 23.7 kg (52.2 lb) when full, with a capacity of 18 litres (4 gallons), this bucket is an almost 'archaeological' illustration of three components of industrial furniture: sheet metal, rustproofing (zinc) and assembly technique (rivets).

DUGDILL LAMP

JOHN DUGDILL / 1907

With a look that is at the same time ancient and avant-garde, these lamps have escaped from the refined atmosphere of collectors' cabinets and are finding their way into stylish modern homes. Similar workshop lamps were manufactured by O.C. White (1883) in America, by Midgard in Germany, by Gras in France and by Dugdill in England (1907). The design of this last is attributed to John Dugdill, an electrical engineer from Manchester, who filed a patent for a 'rotating electrical switch' in 1906. In 1907 the magazine *The Electrical Review* mentioned an invention that improved the coupling pin of working lamps, stopping them from unscrewing themselves and working loose.

John Dugdill was a prolific inventor and filed a succession of technical patents in both Britain and the United States before 1939, all intended to improve the performance of his lamp. The details of its industrial manufacture are still unknown; Dugdill & Co. Ltd was probably founded around 1930.

Examples manufactured before the 1940s are found on the market in both Britain and the United States. This large brass lamp, with a height of 96 cm (37¾ in.) and a base measuring 10.5 cm (4⅛ in.) in diameter, is Edwardian in style although its ornamentation was simplified over the years; the model has adjustable arms made from steel tubing, giving it a style that is pure and clean. Over the course of its evolution, the Dugdill lamp lost its rows of iconic beads, although these were emulated by its American counterpart.

The adjustable Dugdill work lamp has two 32 cm (12⅝ in.) long arms mounted on a cast-iron base, and pivots both vertically and horizontally thanks to its 'daisy-head' adjusting nuts (replaced with a bead in later versions).

The scallop-shaped shade swivels in order to direct the beam of light. The name of Dugdill is stamped on the base. The three holes indicate that this lamp could be mounted on a table or wall.

TEXTILE FACTORY FURNITURE

SINGER / C. 1910

Sewing machines were not the only things manufactured by the world-famous Singer Company. Half a century after having practically monopolized the retail market with its famous invention, Singer launched a range of professional furniture for the textile industry.

In the mid-19th century, Isaac Merritt Singer's American firm invented the hire-purchase system in order to equip as many women as possible. 'Owning a Singer was the ambition of many working women, who would buy them on credit, with a subscription. Many married women hoped to earn some extra money while taking care of their homes.'[1]

Buoyed by its success, Singer took the initiative in 1910 by offering textile manufacturers 'ready-to-use' factories and marketing specially adapted furniture: a stool with a cast-iron base and wooden seat launched the range. Fifteen years later, fitted with a spring and a backrest, it had become an adjustable chair. Chairs, stools and cutting tables suitable for use with machinery would also be produced over the next half century. A Bakelite lamp, jointed in order to shine as precise a light as possible on to the working area, soon joined them; this invention would later inspire such manufacturers as Lumina, Bordas and the German company Pfaff.

1 Michele Perrot, *Histoires de chambres*, Paris, 2009.

The chair had claw feet; its pyramid-shaped base was topped with an adjustable backrest (two different heights were available) supported by two cast-iron arms, later replaced by strips of steel. An adjustable Bakelite lamp was designed to light the working area.

METAL WASTE-PAPER BASKET

From one icon to another: the waste-paper baskets on which Steelcase built an empire have now been supplanted by the virtual trash cans that appear on our computer screens.

METAL OFFICE FURNITURE COMPANY / 1910 / RONÉO FROM 1960

When the Metal Office Furniture Company patented its first invention in the early 20th century, the waste-paper basket played a major role in the office. At that time paper was at the heart of the organization of office life; it carried information and was the link between different posts and levels of hierarchy. Documents were transmitted, sorted, archived or thrown away.

During this period, architects were building offices from bricks and steel, but they were still equipped with wooden furniture. The simple six-sided steel Victor waste-paper basket owes its existence to the fear of fire. It heralded the end of fires caused by careless smokers throwing the ashes of a still-smouldering cigarette into a waste bin full of crumpled paper. Despite its far from graceful appearance – not unlike a plant pot painted to look like wood – it was its promise of durability that led to the Victor waste-paper basket's widespread success. Steelcase, the name later adopted by the Metal Office Furniture Company, went on to develop an entire range of fireproof office furniture.

The visionary US firm offered this waste-paper basket in a variety of different versions, many of which sported the company's name in joyfully listing cursive letters flanked by a 'V', standing proudly with its arms held up to the skies.

It is likely that the Victor model inspired the Ronéo brand in the 1960s to launch on the French market this rectangular metal bin measuring 34 cm (13³/₈ in.) by 28 cm (11 in.).

The lampshade of the Triplex wall light (made from enamelled metal and chrome) is connected to a double swivel joint attached to two telescopic shafts. The lamp rotates through 360 degrees, a feature that has made it popular with the medical profession ever since it was first on the market.[3]

TRIPLEX LAMP

JOHAN PETTER JOHANSSON / 1919 / REISSUED BY MACKAPÄR

This well-designed lamp became a highly prized decorative object during the Roaring Twenties, before being reborn almost a century later thanks to a group of enthusiasts; the story of the Triplex lamp shows no sign of coming to an end.

After learning the trade in a mechanics workshop, the Swedish engineer Johan Petter Johansson (1853–1943) formed his own company when he came up with the idea of creating a tool that would make history: the adjustable spanner. Sold in a shop run by his son, it was soon found around the world. It would not be his sole creation; an inventor of genius, Johansson filed no fewer than 118 patents over the course of his long career, predominantly for tools and tool parts. He went on to become one of the founders of the BAHCO brand, still a market leader in its field.[1] There is a museum dedicated to his work in Enköping, Sweden.

This work lamp was one of Johan Petter Johansson's final designs. In 1919 he opened the Triplex factory, which developed adjustment systems for machine tools, lamps and so on. The Triplex lamp was created in the same year. In 1926 it made the transition into the home thanks to the intervention of the famous Finnish designer and architect Alvar Aalto, who made it a sought-after decorative item.[2]

More than sixty years after Johansson's death, another Swedish engineer, Robert Kullenberg, fell in love

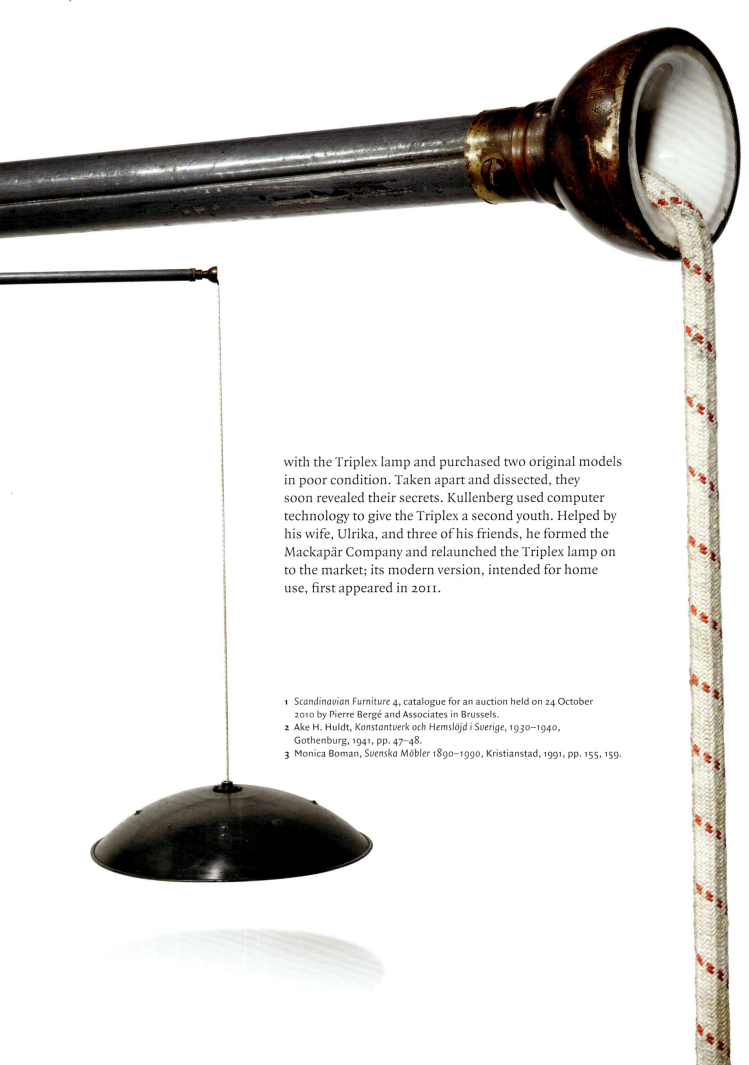

with the Triplex lamp and purchased two original models in poor condition. Taken apart and dissected, they soon revealed their secrets. Kullenberg used computer technology to give the Triplex a second youth. Helped by his wife, Ulrika, and three of his friends, he formed the Mackapär Company and relaunched the Triplex lamp on to the market; its modern version, intended for home use, first appeared in 2011.

1 *Scandinavian Furniture 4*, catalogue for an auction held on 24 October 2010 by Pierre Bergé and Associates in Brussels.
2 Ake H. Huldt, *Konstantverk och Hemslöjd i Sverige, 1930–1940*, Gothenburg, 1941, pp. 47–48.
3 Monica Boman, *Svenska Möbler 1890–1990*, Kristianstad, 1991, pp. 155, 159.

INSPECTION LAMP

UNKNOWN DESIGNER / C. 1920 / STILL IN PRODUCTION

In 2011 the Swedish design studio Form Us With Love brought together hundreds of examples of their 'Work Lamps' for Design House Stockholm, combining them in dazzling installations, proudly flaunting their tangled leads. This barely updated version of the inspection lamp (with a gilded-steel cage and a discreet switch on the base) lights up impromptu events and trendy concept stores, and shines throughout the pages of chic decorating magazines.

Its country of origin and parentage are both unknown; an orphan of the world, the inspection lamp first displayed its useful qualities on farms and in garages, attics, cellars and factories, until it became indispensable. So much so that it still lights up garages and farms, slightly more gracefully than a century ago and considerably more safely.

A triumphant example of 'useful form', the inspection lamp is straightforward and free from any complex components. A cable, a plug, a socket and a bulb, with protective casing made from metal sheeting or iron in a domed or half-shell shape or in the form of a wire cage: only the materials have evolved over time. Now decorated with a plastic or silicon-coated rubber handle, it is also often fitted with a coloured lead (in the workplace the lead stands out clearly against the ground to avoid the risk of an accident). Its bulb no longer heats up, but, undoubtedly for the sake of elegance, it always sports a cover.

The Spanish designer Marti Guixé paid tribute to the lamp with his Cau collection for Danese; a hanging lampshade or table lamp is coupled with an inspection lamp that can be hung inside it in any position. Its bright orange power lead, seemingly taken straight from a building site, can also be wrapped decoratively around the classically styled shade. A cheeky manifesto: from the garage to the lounge, from one century to the next, this nomadic piece of lighting is the perfect illustration of the maxim that 'simple design is good design'.

The first inspection lamps were not without danger, poorly insulated as they were; using them brought with it the risk of burns, and short circuits were not unknown. Some examples dating from the late 19th century were decorated with metalwork cages representative of a certain amount of ancestral know-how originating in Eastern Europe.

METAL KITCHEN CABINET

UNKNOWN DESIGNER / C. 1920

Metal kitchen units began to appear at the end of the First World War. The 1918 Spanish Flu epidemic left thirty million victims in its wake worldwide; hygiene and health became the new battleground of governments in countries weakened by war and disease. This was the era of the sanitary kitchen, of porcelain, enamelled surfaces and bare floors (linoleum gained ground on floor tiles); everything had to be non-perishable and easy to clean, or rather to disinfect. White and lighter-coloured shades established themselves as symbols of purity and health.

A hygienic alternative to the pantries of days gone by, which were poorly equipped to resist rodents, maggots, weevils, damp or heat, metal units were resistant to vermin. Metal furniture makers also offered tables, sideboards and storage cabinets to match.

In the United States, the Indiana-based Hoosier Manufacturing Company came up with the idea in 1898 of equipping a traditional pantry cupboard to turn it into a proper 'pastry-making unit'.[1] These were fitted with a metal reservoir for flour that was adjustable and could contain more than 20 kg (44 lb); housewives used them by operating a built-in sieve. A sugar container and a bread drawer were also made of sheet metal to preserve the foodstuffs. The Hoosier Cabinet had a number of tricks (including a spice rack and turntables). Its success was such that in the early 20th century the majority of American homes had a Hoosier: the name became generic and was used to refer both to Hoosier products and to those of its competitors.

In the 1920s and 1930s, such firms as Whitehead, Servel, Elgin and De Dietrich continued to use sheet metal, but then began to sell fitted kitchen units, often equipped with an electric refrigerator. Free-standing cabinets, made from sheet metal or lined with tin, gradually disappeared.

1 Nancy R. Hiller, *The Hoosier Cabinet in Kitchen History*, Bloomington, IN, 2009.

The two-door kitchen cabinet, made from white lacquered sheet steel and with a functional layout, appeared in mail-order catalogues under the name 'all-in-one cabinet' until the 1960s; its ergonomic design and its price in particular guaranteed it an unusually long life.

'HOMEMADE' LAMP

UNKNOWN DESIGNER / C. 1920–40

'The new factory started out small, with some steel-toed boots, a cutting machine, a single nickel vat and three workers.'[1] When a factory was opened in 1890, the question of 'workplace furniture' did not arise. And for good reason: at that time, space was devoted only to machinery. Raw materials and manufactured objects were just left on the floor.

But shortly a box or two would be added, and soon a workbench and a vice arrive. In the hands of craftsmen, scrap wood and metal, unwanted household objects and all sorts of other items could be recycled and transformed into 'tools' tailored for every job.

Some years later, with the advent of electricity, the first workshop lamps were created as part of this domestic economy, with sockets hanging from wires and makeshift metal cones as shades. The arrival of new machinery with more complicated workings would one day lead a man to weld a more suitable model on to a corner of his workbench. And because he 'crafted it himself, modified it, transformed it, in short he made it to measure, he became one with it'.[2]

Made by hand and used by hand, unique tools such as these bear witness to the history of the working world and have become part of an exclusive group of folk objects. They can now be found in museums or specialist antique shops.

1 Jean Anglade, *Les Ventres jaunes*, Paris, 1979.
2 Robert Linhart, *L'Établi*, Paris, 1978.

This mid-20th-century lamp incorporates the bare minimum of parts: three 34 cm (13⅜ in.) steel tubes linked with U-shaped iron pieces; a riveted and welded steel shade (the interior was galvanized to reflect the light); and a clamp to mount the lamp on a workbench. The lamp can be extended to a length of 112 cm (44 in.) and can be moved up and down and from left to right.

STRAFOR SHELVING 1521

FORGES DE STRASBOURG / 1920

'Because it is in the national interest': this appeal to purchase French steel appeared in the preface to the first catalogue from Strafor, the Forges de Strasbourg brand, in 1920. The sales pitch concluded, 'we must seek out opportunities for metal and look for new ways to use steel in all fields of industrial activity, including the manufacture of metal furniture.'

At that time Forges de Strasbourg was the leading producer of steel furniture and shelving in Europe. Equipped with rolling machines, it began to specialize in the production of high-quality thin and corrugated sheet metal. Behind this metal shelving unit, a symbolic piece of workplace furniture, lies the story of a French company that, in the 1920s, owned three factories occupying 24 hectares (59 acres) and had 1,300 employees and a business that stretched across France and beyond.

Forges de Strasbourg retained its pioneer status until 1974, when it went into partnership with the American firm Steelcase.[1] Although part of the same industry as the Alsace company, Steelcase brought other valuable skills; the French brand hoped to add seating, Steelcase's flagship product, to its catalogue, and opened a factory in Sarrebourg. Strafor also successfully took on the task of fitting out service-industry sites, benefiting from its associate's network to build an international reputation.

The 1521 Strafor shelving unit calls to mind two characteristics of the period from which it originated: the frenzied consumption of paper and an obsession with storage. Like all shelving units and lockers by this firm, it is made of corrugated sheet metal. An oval plaque fixed to the base bears the inscription 'Strafor, Forges de Strasbourg.' This four-shelf unit is 215 cm (84⅝ in.) high, 100 cm (39⅜ in.) wide and 30 cm (11¾ in.) deep.

1 Steelcase Strafor (whose capital was provided equally by both original companies) was formed in 1981. In 1999 Steelcase Strafor became Steelcase International and is a publicly traded company under the acronym 'SCS.'

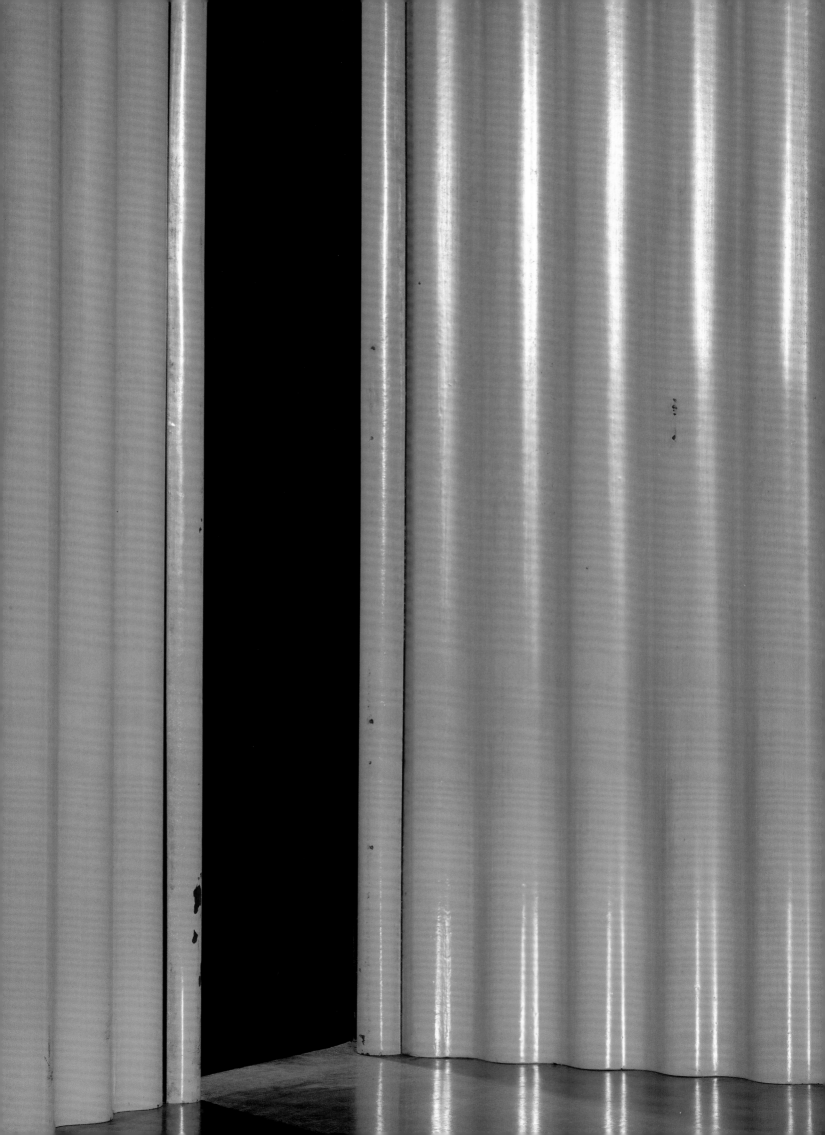

BIENAISE CHAIR

NELSON BROTHERS / 1921

The Bienaise chair, the Mappemonde architect's table, American system chairs and terrace chairs from Multipl's and Tolix, as well as Midgard, Triplex and Gras lamps, all bore witness to the prospects now offered by metalwork and the consequences to which it pointed. Stackable and adjustable in a way that wood could never allow, the furniture of the Industrial Revolution opened the way for the science of ergonomics.

The first specially designed office chair in France, the Bienaise came into being in the early 1920s. Known for a long time only from rare early examples, it is now much sought-after. Originals, bearing the engraved and riveted plaque reading 'SIEGE BIENAISE Breveté SGDG', make extremely rare appearances on the market and enthusiasts have to content themselves with models produced in the 1960s and 1970s.

The origins of the brand lie with two brothers, Frank and Harry Nelson, who left Michigan to settle in Paris. From the 1920s onwards, in their studio in the 15th arrondissement, they made bicycle saddles and

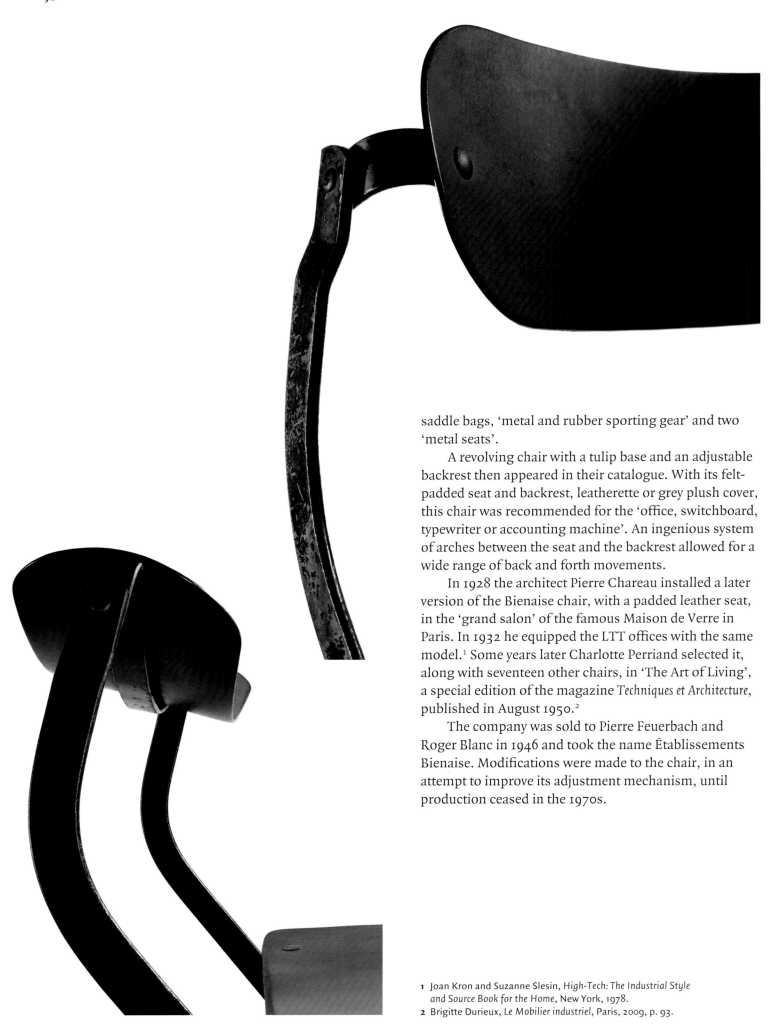

saddle bags, 'metal and rubber sporting gear' and two 'metal seats'.

A revolving chair with a tulip base and an adjustable backrest then appeared in their catalogue. With its felt-padded seat and backrest, leatherette or grey plush cover, this chair was recommended for the 'office, switchboard, typewriter or accounting machine'. An ingenious system of arches between the seat and the backrest allowed for a wide range of back and forth movements.

In 1928 the architect Pierre Chareau installed a later version of the Bienaise chair, with a padded leather seat, in the 'grand salon' of the famous Maison de Verre in Paris. In 1932 he equipped the LTT offices with the same model.[1] Some years later Charlotte Perriand selected it, along with seventeen other chairs, in 'The Art of Living', a special edition of the magazine *Techniques et Architecture*, published in August 1950.[2]

The company was sold to Pierre Feuerbach and Roger Blanc in 1946 and took the name Établissements Bienaise. Modifications were made to the chair, in an attempt to improve its adjustment mechanism, until production ceased in the 1970s.

1 Joan Kron and Suzanne Slesin, *High-Tech: The Industrial Style and Source Book for the Home*, New York, 1978.
2 Brigitte Durieux, *Le Mobilier industriel*, Paris, 2009, p. 93.

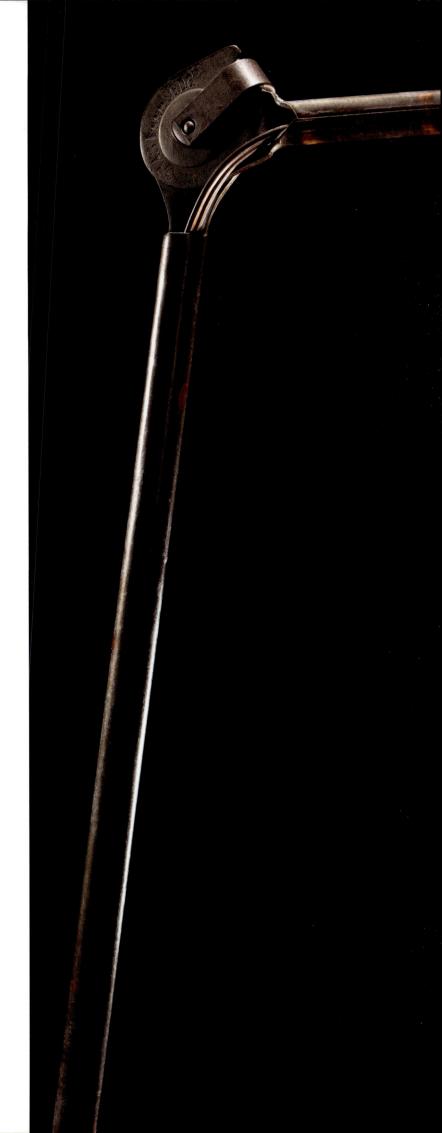

GRAS LAMP

....

BERNARD-ALBIN GRAS / 1921

....

The ancestor of all adjustable French lamps, the Gras lamp was first produced in the 1920s and has had an exemplary career without even the slightest modification in half a century.

Functionality guides the simplicity of its aesthetic; neither solder nor screws are on display. The secret of this 'adjustable lamp for industrial use' (as described in its patent dating from October 1921) lies in its at first flat, then hollow, connecting rod, the famous arm with jointed ends that contains the electrical cable.

The partnership between Bernard-Albin Gras and Louis-Didier des Gachons, at the head of the Industrie du Tourniquet et du Classeur (Revolving Rack and Cabinet Manufacturer), allowed the Gras lamp to make a name for itself in a market that was experiencing a boom in the service sector. Since its creation, twenty-three models with seven different shades have appeared in the catalogue in order to respond to the needs of the greatest possible number of professionals.

Stamped with RAVEL from 1927 (taken from the name of the associate of Louis-Didier des Gachons), the adjustable lamp was used to light architects' tables and artists' studios as well as machine tools.

On a mahogany base, this unique model (part of the Louis-Didier des Gachons production) has an 'extended' double pagoda lampshade. The metal body is covered with 'gun barrel' polish, which, reworked by hand, reveals the underlying red copper.

The big names of the period would do much for its popularity, including Le Corbusier (who used it in his offices and then put it in the buildings he designed), Robert Mallet-Stevens, Jacques Ruhlmann, Eileen Gray, Sonia Delaunay and Georges Braque. In the 1950s, competition – from the Jieldé lamp in particular – eventually got the better of the Gras lamp, and production was halted in the early 1970s.

In 2008 Philippe Cazer and Frédéric Winkler formed the DCW Company and reissued the Gras lamp. Whether a question of old models for collectors or newly reissued models, Bernard-Albin Gras's perennially acclaimed invention can consider itself proud to have played an iconic role in the history of lighting.

MULTIPL'S CHAIRS AND TABLE

JOSEPH MATHIEU / 1922

The table is 72 cm (28³/₈ in.) high with a top measuring 62.5 cm (24³/₅ in.) by 80 cm (31½ in.). The table and the seat of the chair are no longer welded in the traditional way, but the various elements fit neatly one inside the other. This is therefore a later version of the design, from which Multipl's seems to have taken inspiration from Tolix.

Frequently confused with the Model A chair by Xavier Pauchard (the two models competed on the market during the interwar period), the Multipl's chair can be recognized by the concave shape of its legs.

This metal chair, designed by Joseph Mathieu in Lyons in 1922 and manufactured by the industrial furniture company Multipl's, quickly became a force to be reckoned with in the world of outdoor furniture, on café terraces, in public gardens and in the smart restaurants of spa resorts and the Riviera. It could also be found in factory canteens and hospitals.

A quarter of a century earlier, steam-bent wood designs by the Thonet brothers or Kohn reigned supreme in the same locations, but these light, non-perishable and most importantly stackable metal chairs soon took their place. Joseph Mathieu, one of the masters of this revolution, was soon selling a complete range consisting of chairs, stools and tables.

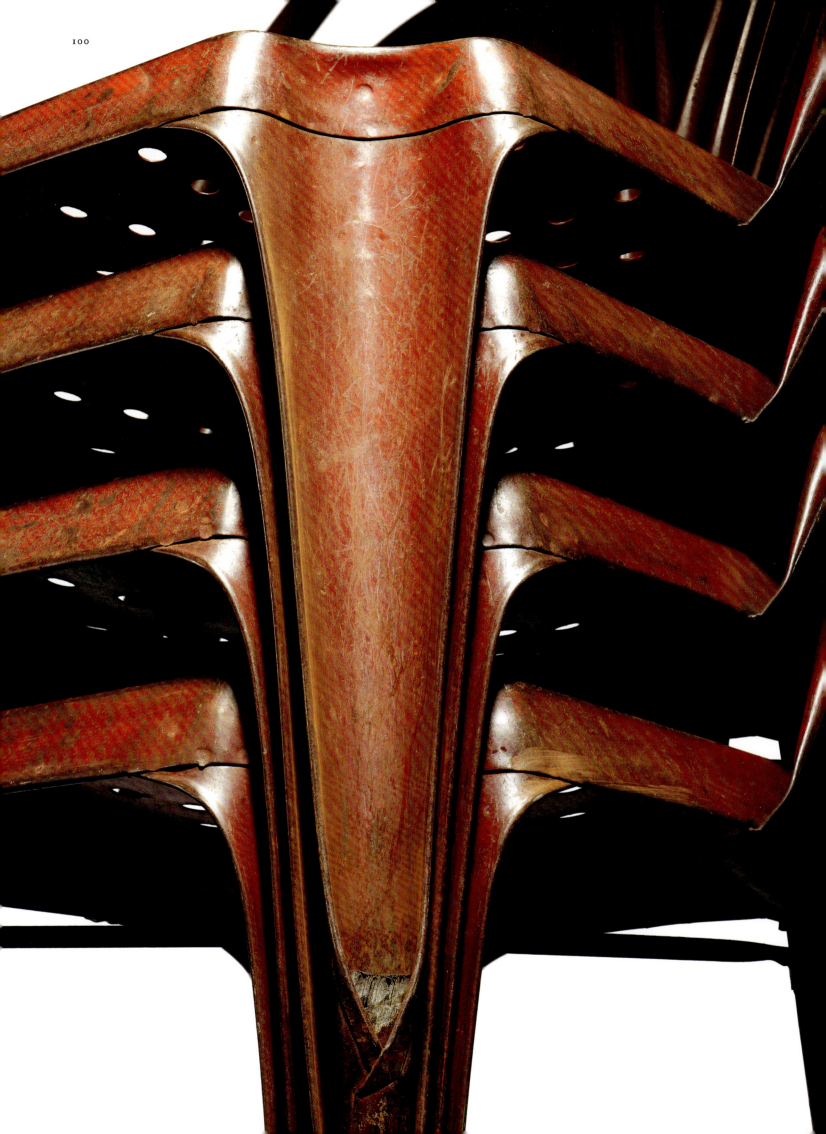

The origin of the chair is as complex as a game of Meccano; twenty pieces of stamped sheet steel were shaped and assembled (including eight pieces for the seat, four for the legs and five for the backrest).

Sheet metal soon became popular with both commercial and individual clients, but its manufacture remained artisanal. The multiple die-stamped pieces that made up the chair and the considerable amount of welding involved made its production even harder to mechanize.

The originality of its design led the organizers of the 1928 Stuttgart exhibition to shortlist the chair alongside creations from designers such as Marcel Breuer, Ludwig Mies van der Rohe and Mart Stam. In 1969, three Multipl's chairs received a supreme accolade when they appeared in the painting *Ossie Clark and Peter Schlesinger at Le Parc des Sources, Vichy* by David Hockney. Making them the focal point of this work, Hockney invites the viewer to take a seat on the single chair that is left empty for this very purpose.

Ste Meubles MULTIPL'S
Brevetés et Déposés
LYON
30 Rue Servient
FABRIQUÉ EN FRANCE

MIDGARD 113 LAMP

CURT FISCHER / C. 1923 / REISSUED IN 2005

The German factory Ronneberger & Fischer, in Auma, specialized in the manufacture of industrial machinery for ceramicists (potters' wheels and various other tools). In 1922 the engineer Curt Fischer, who was unhappy with the lighting in the workshops, designed an adjustable lamp that could be fitted on to a work table. It was christened Midgard. In Norse mythology this is the name given to the fortification constructed all the way around the world, and was intended in this case as a reference to the zone that the lamp was to illuminate.

Curt Fischer developed a complete range of lighting from 1923 onwards: telescopic, ceiling and wall-mounted lights, floor lamps and lamps fitted with ingenious vice-grips as well as variations intended for domestic use (a lamp for a desk or for lighting needlework) and industrial use (machine tools). An extendible scissor version, a variation of the wall bracket, met with great success. The Midgard lamp was also admired for its lines. Bauhaus professors in Weimar required their students to use this ideal working lamp, praising its design, its slender 'neck' and the original shape of its bias-cut shade. Walter Gropius, the founder of the school, adopted the Midgard in his home.[1] Marianne Brandt, head of the Metal workshop at the school, admitted that she had always regretted not having designed it herself, 'even if our lamps were adjustable, they were not as elegant, and we envied the designer of the Midgard lamp.'[2]

The Midgard 113 lamp with its original colouring. It is fitted with a jointed arm and a bevelled aluminium rotating shade bearing the inscription 'MIDGARD DRGM' as well as the company logo. At the time, customers could choose between twelve different shades available in the catalogue.

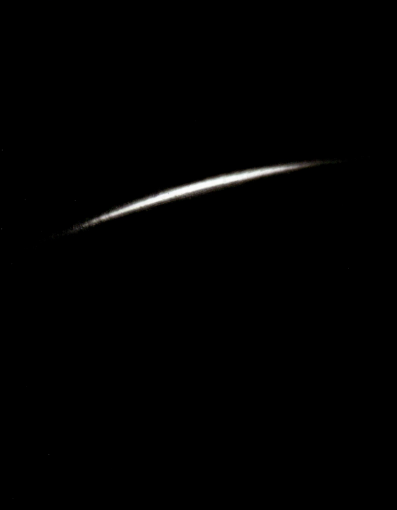

The fate of this lamp is linked to that of Germany. When Curt Fischer died, his son Wolfgang took over the company, which was subject to a compulsory purchase order in 1971. Renamed VEB-Raumleuchte, it now owns three factories and manufactures public lighting. It has up to 500 employees and, most notably, produces extendible lamps for IKEA.

The Midgard brand was protected by patents, however; privatized once again in 1990, the company became Midgard Licht SARL. In 2002 Wolfgang Fischer sold the company to his stepdaughters, Anja Falkje and Susi Reifenstahl. In 2005 they reissued 200 of the Midgard-Lenklampen Type 113 and Type 114 models, and won a design award.[3] The 2008 financial crisis led to the closure of the factory, which went into liquidation in 2011; the two 'heiresses' are currently hoping that a buyer can be found to keep the brand alive.

1 Franz Fühmann, *Die Metallwerkstatt am Bauhaus*, Berlin, 1992.
2 'Beneidet haben wir später die Erfinder des Armes der Midgardleuchte – unsere Lampe war zwar auch verstellbar, aber eben nicht so elegant.' Source: http://www.midgard-licht.de
3 The Thüringen Design Award, 2005.

TOLIX MODEL A CHAIR

XAVIER PAUCHARD / 1925

Found on the terraces of the bistros of the interwar period, on the sets of early 21st-century television programmes, in the collections of the Vitra Design Museum, and from MoMA to the Pompidou Centre: Xavier Pauchard's Model A chair (1880–1948) is an undisputed symbol of a great industrial heritage that is the true heir to traditional skills and craftsmanship.

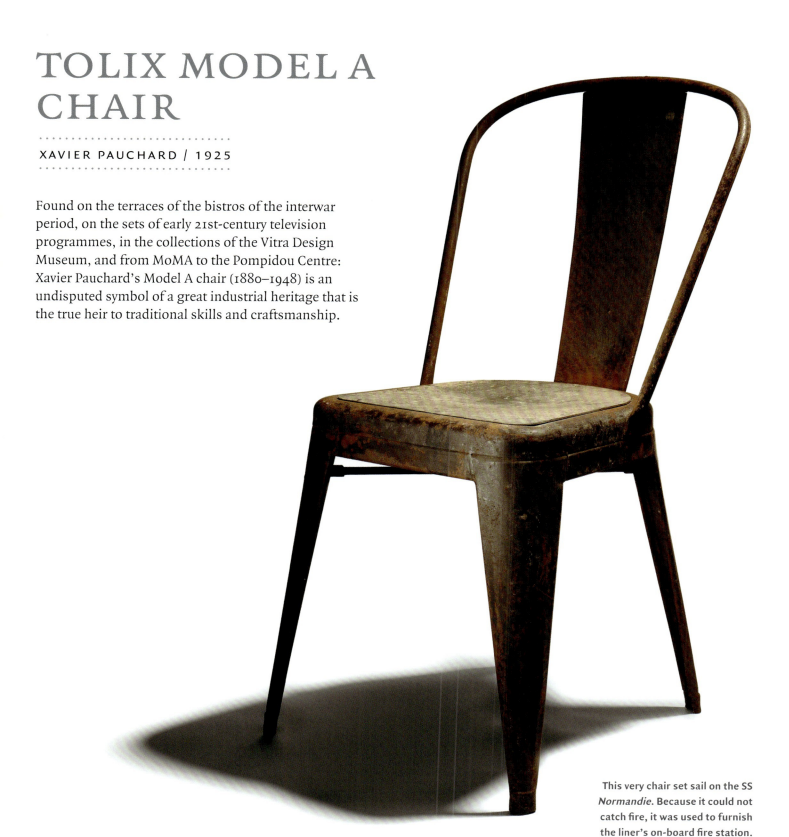

This very chair set sail on the SS Normandie. Because it could not catch fire, it was used to furnish the liner's on-board fire station.

Over the course of the trials carried out in Xavier Pauchard's workshops in Autun, a prototype was perfected in the 1920s. It was a significant moment; the appearance of the chair designed by this Burgundian craftsman marked a turning point, and its influence would prove to be long-lasting. By relying on his 'faultless mastery of material and technique', Xavier Pauchard succeeded where, according to Serge Lemoine, the key exponents of Bauhaus had failed.[1] Rationalism, functionality and aesthetics are combined in a chair, which, unlike its predecessors, could be mass-produced. Its production process anticipated the 'one-piece' concept that would become the norm with the advent of moulded plastic.

The earliest examples did not yet have ridged legs, which were fitted with steel runners. Some thought the ridging was what made the chair stackable, but in fact, this improvement was intended to make the legs, which were prone to buckling, more rigid – a problem that the Lyon-based company Multipl's was unable to overcome.

For more than a half century, Tolix furniture was rarely marked with the company name. Exceptions include the chairs made for the luxury liner SS *Normandie*, which are identifiable thanks to the round label affixed to the reverse of the backrest, bearing the inscription 'Les sièges métalliques Tolix Autun'. When Chantal Andriot took over the reins at Tolix in 2004, she added clear branding to every item that leaves the workshops.

1 Former president of the Musée d'Orsay in Paris; quoted in Brigitte Durieux, *Inoxydable Tolix*, Paris, 2008.

FLAMBO CHAIR

HENRI LIBER / 1926

The typist's chair was invented in the United States right at the end of the 19th century, thirty years after the birth of the typewriter. The Flambo chair did not arrive in France until the interwar period. This height-adjustable swivel chair owes its originality to a hairpin spring, the invention of a man called Henri Liber, nicknamed 'Monsieur Flambo' after he created a small light that lit up when turned. The Société Flambo was formed in 1919. Trained in industrial design, in 1926 Henri Liber began to sell a chair that became an important addition to his range of office supplies, which included Papic drawing pins, still available today.[1] He also devised the Roule-Dactyle system, consisting of chairs that rolled along rails in front of desks and storage cabinets.

Henri Liber continued to improve the ergonomics of his chair; in 1927 a coiled spring allowed the backrest to rock, and he supplemented it with a foam rubber cushion. The Flambo M42 chair was born.

The French manufacturer proudly displayed his furniture in the 'French Office' pavilion at the International Exhibition in Paris in 1937, proving that French production was worth its salt in terms of ingenuity and strength when compared to its foreign competitors, including designs produced in Germany.

The company flourished; under the Nazi occupation the workshop at Fontenay-sous-Bois was abandoned in favour of Nogent-le-Roi, after which a finishing and storage centre was set up in Saint-Denis in the early 1960s. Flambo numbered 1,000 or so employees when, in 1968, Michel, the son of Henri Liber, became head of a factory in Vierzon, bringing some 700 employees with him. But crisis was to come, two decades later; the company went into liquidation in 1986.

1 See Yolande Amic, *L'Empire du bureau 1900–2000*, Paris, 1984.

The Flambo chair was the creation of a prolific inventor: Henri Liber filed more than 100 patents. Specialists maintain that it can be identified by its manufacturer's mark: its oblong washers. It is fitted with Bakelite-tipped legs; the backrest and the seat were originally fitted with leather or velvet pads.

RONÉO TABLE

· · · · · · · · · · · · · · · · · · · ·

RONÉO / C. 1927

· · · · · · · · · · · · · · · · · · · ·

Four legs, casters, a tabletop; nothing about this table is particularly extraordinary, apart from its provenance: the Salon Rose of the Villa Saint-Bernard in Hyères belonging to the Vicomte de Noailles. Designed largely by Robert Mallet-Stevens between 1924 and 1931, the villa was one of the first modern houses in France in terms of not only its architecture but also its furnishings. Added in 1927, the drawing room is filled almost exclusively with metal furniture, some of which was attributed to the Ronéo brand by Léon Deshairs in the magazine *Art et Décoration* (July 1928). This factory had already received praise from Le Corbusier in his book *The Decorative Art of Today* (1925), for the aesthetic and functional qualities of the items it produced. The famous architect had himself paved the way for the introduction of furniture from the working world, both the factory and the office, into the domestic sphere.

No catalogue or patent survives confirming Deshairs's attribution. Was this then a specific commission designed by the architect? It is unlikely; the design is heavy and not particularly inventive. However, the machine-pressed steel used and the quality of the welding point towards experienced execution. The role of Mallet-Stevens consisted mainly of choosing creations by such designers as Breuer, Chareau and Perriand and combining them; the Ronéo tables, the Gras lamps and the legs of the Smith chairs are all painted in the same Duco mid-grey. This fired lacquer, designed for the bodywork of cars, bears witness to the willingness to use industrial processes on everyday furniture.

The above text was contributed by Stéphane Boudin-Lestienne, Doctor of Art History and Architecture, historian at the Villa Noailles.

Small side table on casters for the Salon Rose of the Villa Saint-Bernard in Hyères belonging to the Vicomte de Noailles, 1927. Collection of the Villa Noailles, purchased with the assistance of the Saint-Bernard Friends Association in 2009 and restored by Marc Hotermans in 2010.

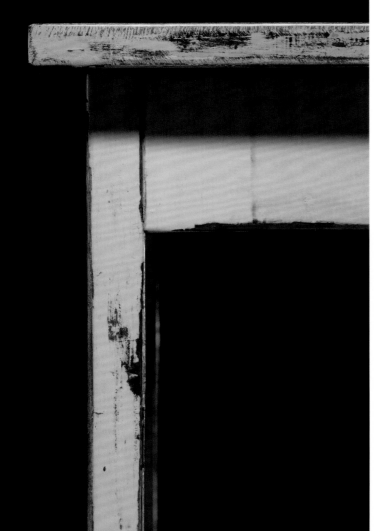

GALAXIE FLOODLIGHT

SOCIÉTÉ FRANÇAISE D'ÉCLAIRAGE GAL / 1928

This floodlight measures 100 cm (39⅜ in.) in diameter and is fitted with a 1,000-watt mercury vapour lamp creating a narrow but far-reaching beam, perfect for use on railways. Its brightness is linked not to the wattage of the bulb but to the geometric properties of the parabolic curves. SNCF installed this light along the tracks in groups of between two and sixteen.

In the 1950s, Longeau (Amiens) was the largest rail yard in Europe. Some 300 railway workers were employed at its shunting stations. Mechanics, train drivers, brakemen, banksmen, lamplighters and pointsmen dealt with thousands of tons of freight from booming post-war France. For a long time prior to that, lamps and candles had no longer been enough to guarantee the productivity and safety of those carrying out night-time work. So the French rail company SNCF turned to its supplier, the lighting company GAL,[1] and the Galaxie floodlight was born. Encouraged by trials carried out at their central laboratory at Saint-Ouen, the SNCF building fixtures department approved a design. The body, made from thick sheet steel and weighing 32 kg (70 lb), and an ultrapure aluminium mirror were carried by a steel stirrup that pivoted and swung on a moulded cast-iron base. Additionally it incorporated the astonishing 100-cm-long (39⅜ in.) reflector shade that was mounted on pylons, 20 m (65 ft 6 in.) high.

1 The Société Française d'Éclairage, GAL, formed in Courbevoie in the 1930s, was taken over by Bruneau Charnay in 2002.

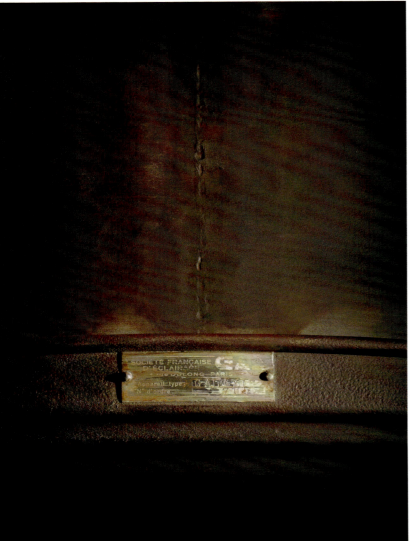
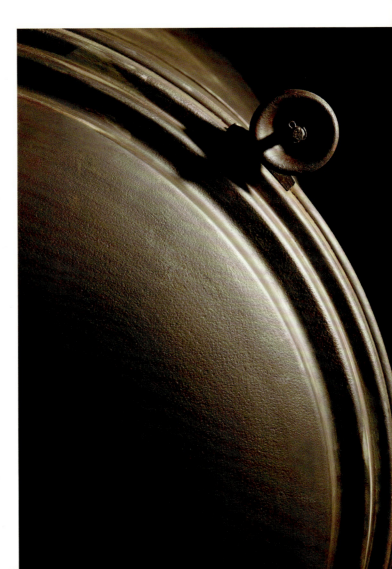

MODEL 9 PEDESTAL TABLE AND A56 CHAIR

XAVIER AND JEAN PAUCHARD / C. 1930 AND 1956

Making space profitable, putting as many drinks as possible on the tables and optimizing the back-and-forth journeys of the waiters: turning café terraces into profitable businesses was the Pauchard family credo. And for good reason; brewers were demanding clients and they represented the largest share of the Pauchards' turnover. The profit generated enabled the company to finance its own equipment: 'The truckloads of thousands of chairs that left the factory for the La Comète brewery in Châlons-sur-Marne allowed us to purchase the metal-bending machine.'

Father and son continued to perfect their designs, with varying degrees of success. This was the case with two of Xavier Pauchard's early creations: the non-stackable Model B and Model E chairs, or the hastily issued Model G table, which was described as capable of being taken apart and reassembled but in reality was impossible to stack owing to its weight. The two manufacturers kept an eye on the competition by listening to the feedback delivered by their representatives at a meeting held every season at the factory in Autun.

Unlike its primary competitor, Multipl's, which reissued the same design over and over again, the Tolix brand produced a growing range of chairs and tables, allowing its customers to choose from the catalogue according to their requirements and constraints, whether financial or aesthetic.

Over time, different shapes came together: the Model 9 pedestal table by Xavier Pauchard and the A56 chairs by his son Jean were designed twenty-five years apart, but matched each other comfortably. The pedestal table's edged top could accommodate four glasses of beer and their mats, four coffees, plus an ashtray and bill saucer. The cast-iron base was hidden under the table; the chairs were stackable; and café terraces suddenly became a lot more profitable!

Jean Pauchard, head of the Tolix Company that was founded in 1954, six years after the death of his father, was the designer of the A56 chair, which is still on sale today. Twenty-five of these could be stacked together and still measure less than 2.3 m (7 ft 6 in.) in height. This chair was created in response to remarks made by café owners about the Tolix Model C and D chairs, which they thought were too bulky, reducing the space for tables and resulting in a drop in customers. 'I just added an extra backrest section to the Model A chair, and, as it was 1956, I named it the A56.'

British design guru Terence Conran had long been an admirer of Xavier Pauchard's Model A chair, believing it to be such a perfect creation that he assumed it was an American design like the aluminium Navy Chair.[1] He spotted Jean Pauchard's A56 chair and sold it in his Habitat stores. This was a milestone for the brand as the iconic chair was then adopted the world over.

1 Brigitte Durieux, *Inoxydable Tolix*, Paris, 2008, p. 53.

Given its limited production, tables such as this rarely come on to the market. Some examples were recently sold at an auction of furnishings from the EPDI classrooms.

TOUS SENS
BRACKET LAMP

UNKNOWN DESIGNER / C. 1930

With its shaped steel tubing and conical shade, this *grande dame* of the steel world hides several major technological innovations, such as the ball joint and the flexible hose, behind its apparently simple exterior. In the world of industrial French lamps, the Tous Sens comes between the Gras lamp (see page 95), to which it owes a great deal, and the Jieldé lamp (see page 207), which it prefigures.

It is likely that it began to appear in the 1930s; the nascent mechanical industry had need of accurate lighting. It continued to be manufactured until the 1950s, as evidenced by its component parts: the original steel shade gave way to a stamped aluminium model, and the originally cast-iron ball joints were also later made from aluminium.

In order to be adaptable to various work stations and machine tools, the lamp was available in two versions: the bracket version with two asymmetrical arms measuring 50 cm (19⅝ in.) and 20 cm (7⅞ in.), and the mounted version, recognizable thanks to its 90-degree tube and to its three arms, rather than two, which allowed it to be fixed to the wall or directly on to the machine tool.

Both versions of the lamp were marked either with the initials 'TS' or with the words 'Tous Sens' ('Every Direction') on the fixing plate. The TS had all the qualities of greatness. Its only flaw was that the friction of the wire inside the ball joint presented a risk of electrocution. By inventing switches for the Jieldé lamp in the 1950s, Jean-Louis Domecq consigned to history this primitive lamp, the creator and manufacturer of which is still unknown.

The Tous Sens lamp is simultaneously rotating, telescopic, jointed and flexible.

Rotating: two butterfly nuts, bent at an angle to provide grip, allow it to rotate up to 360 degrees.

Telescopic: the same screws allow the bracket to go up and down by around 30 cm (11¾ in.) according to requirements.

Flexible: a spring on the shade fitted with a key socket allows the beam of light to be directed.

Accessories: an electric socket fits under the grip attachment, allowing it to be connected to electric tools.

NICOLLE STOOL

ÉTABLISSEMENTS NICOLLE / 1933

From 1913, Établissements Nicolle, based in Montreuil, specialized in the manufacture of washers. They had a stamping and punching workshop in which they designed the Nicolle stool for their own use and for that of some of their neighbouring factories in 1933. It had three stamped metal legs and a seat in the shape of a large washer.

Soon afterwards they added a backrest, which was compared after the war to the 'tail of a whale'. The stool later became stackable and a fourth leg was added to increase its stability. Soon it was bought and used in factories all over France. It was available in eight different heights, ranging from 45 cm (17¾ in.) to 80 cm (31½ in.), making it suitable for use with many different kinds of machinery.

In 1954 Établissements Nicolle designed two different models of stool with adjustable screws: the 45/60 and the 60/80.

In the early 1960s the company was sold to an American group and the former foreman, Pierre Maurice Félix, started his own business. He resumed the manufacture of the Nicolle stool, the marketing of which was entrusted to Manutan. The dominance of Nicolle stools within French industry then continued. The all-metal designs were fitted with flat cork seats, and later also with wooden seats. However, a new law, requiring that swivel seats used for working at machinery should have five-legged bases, signalled the death of the Nicolle stool.

Jérôme Lepert, a Paris-based antiques dealer specializing in 20th-century industrial furniture, noticed the Nicolle stool in the pages of an old catalogue; setting out in search of its manufacturer, he eventually discovered the moulds, stored in a shed. After having been sold by Monsieur Félix, the company had gone into receivership. Lepert put himself forward as the purchaser of this valuable piece of equipment and restarted production in 2008 in the former factory. The press was reconditioned, the tools restored and the first stools left the workshop.

Now brightly coloured, the Nicolle stool has been the star of interiors magazines and boutiques ever since.

This is a small table from the Nicolle range. Straight out of the factory workers' changing rooms, where its diminutive stature had kept it hidden, it is just 40 cm (15¾ in.) in diameter and 30 cm (11⅞ in.) high. Perhaps, like its recently reissued 'brothers', it will soon be reissued.

ANGLEPOISE LAMP

GEORGE CARWARDINE / 1934

From an industrial region of England to the rue du Faubourg-Saint-Honoré in Paris, the success story of this jointed lamp is stitched in linen thread.

The British industrialist George Carwardine (1887–1948), who designed vehicle suspension systems, invented an extendible spring in 1932 and came up with the idea of using it for a jointed lamp. Inspired by the movements of the human arm, this lamp was mounted on to tubes on which four of the famous springs allowed it to hold its position. The first version of the Anglepoise lamp was issued in 1934.

From 1955 onwards, Anglepoise lamps and Gras lamps were installed on the workbenches of the workshops at the Maison Hermès; their ergonomics responded perfectly to the requirements of this world in which accuracy and the quality of each movement were essential. The Anglepoise was fitted with a shade that allowed the beam of light to be concentrated on precise points without causing glare; and without consuming too much energy, it lit the inside of bags, luggage and briefcases as well as the work of goldsmiths.

Legend has it that a craftsman who was concerned about damaging the leather on which he was working, had the idea of upholstering the cast-iron base of the lamp. Robert Dumas-Hermès (1898–1978), who was running the firm at the time, noticed this leather cover

This is an Anglepoise 1209 lamp dating from 1934, one of the first issued by the British brand. It can be recognized by its funnel-shaped base and four springs. It belongs to the collections of the Hermès Conservatoire des Créations in Pantin and bears the inscription 'The ANGLEPOISE pat. in U.K. and abroad Made in England Herbert Terry and Sons LTD Redditch'. 'Hermès Paris' can be seen in gold letters on one of the panels of the base.

and included it as part of the collection in order to share it with his customers.

George Carwardine's lamp thus became 'dressed' by Hermès: the base was covered in full-grain leather, chosen for its solidity and ease of upkeep, while the underside had rougher leather stretched over it to stop it from slipping. It appeared in the 1954 Hermès catalogue as item no. 612,[1] and was sold as part of an office set including a desk blotter, blotting paper, ashtray, pencil holder and tray, available in coloured calfskin, Moroccan leather or exotic materials such as crocodile skin.

1 The catalogue, published in March and September by the Maison Hermès and entitled *Le Monde d'Hermès* (The World of Hermès), displays the fashion house's collections of prêt-à-porter ladies- and menswear, as well as leather, silk and lifestyle accessories.

LA MOUETTE CHILDREN'S FURNITURE

XAVIER PAUCHARD / 1935

This garden furniture set is a rare, even unique, example of the metal items that were designed for children in the 1930s. Only one full set is currently recorded. The chair was displayed in the 'L'Aveu catégorique de la matière' exhibition at the Villa Noailles in Hyères in July 2006. Another was auctioned in 2010 at the 'Design for Kids' auction in Brussels (Pierre Bergé and Associates).

La Mouette is a small set of garden furniture for children that includes two chairs and a table, issued as a limited edition at Autun during the 1930s by Établissements Xavier Pauchard, under the Tolix brand.

The origins of these creations lie in a question that Xavier Pauchard often used to ask himself, namely, how do we use up our scrap metal? With this in mind he designed an entire children's range to go alongside this set of three: a spade; a rake, spade and pickaxe set called 'The Little Gardener'; and a metal wheelbarrow.

However, it appears that these designs intended for children may have presented a danger, and their manufacture was halted.

Weighing 2.3 kg (5 lb), this chair is a miniature reproduction of the Model C chair, with one small difference: the armrest has only one line of tubing rather than two. Its frame is really that of the seat section of the Tolix stool. The folded metalwork is of note, including the detail of the folded edges, the open riveting on the crosspiece and the folded steel runners.

The pedestal table is 55.5 cm (21⅞ in.) high and consists of a round cast-iron base and a stamped top, 39.5 cm (15½ in.) in diameter, and is typical of Pauchard's furniture designs. Also notable is the folded metal edging of the tabletop, which remains one of the hallmarks of this Burgundy-based firm.

LUXO LAMP

JACOB JACOBSEN / 1938

With sales of more than twenty-five million, the Luxo lamp, still in production and now on display at MoMA in New York, shows no signs of disappearing.

The Norwegian engineer Jacob Jacobsen (1901–96), an importer of machine tools for the textile industry, was given an Anglepoise 1227 lamp in 1936. Struck by the object's design and ingenuity, he bought a licence to manufacture it in Scandinavia and then redesigned it by simplifying its forms. Made in Oslo, the Luxo L-1, named from a Latin word meaning 'giver of light', was officially released in 1938. Soon it was being used in schools, offices, industrial workshops, healthcare facilities, and design and architect's studios, until it completely took over from the Anglepoise. In the 1940s it was the most commonplace working lamp in both Europe and the United States.

In the 1960s the Italian firm Naska Loris seems to have been the recipient of a distribution licence for the Luxo; a number of these models are often found in the hands of antiquarians. The Italian company Fontana Arte acquired Naska Loris in 1996 and in turn marketed the lamp under the name Naska.

The timeless lines of the Luxo have inspired some of the world's greatest designers. In 1971, Gaetano Pesce gave it a stature consistent with its status as a 'giant of design' by creating the Moloch Floor Lamp, manufactured by Bracciodiferro and reaching an amazing 2.86 m (9 ft 4 in.) in height. In 2011 the German designer Stefan Geisbauer created a two-dimensional tribute to the lamp for Ingo Maurer GmbH; the Looksoflat Lamp is a flattened but functional version of Luxo, fitted with LEDs.

The only thing Luxo lacked was the ability to speak. Although he stopped short of making it talk, animator John Lasseter took inspiration from his own desk lamp and turned a minature version of it into the star of one of the earliest computer-generated cartoons, *Luxo Jr.*, created with the agreement of Jacob Jacobsen. The character of Luxo Jr went on to become the logo of Pixar Studios.[1]

1 In 2009, Luxo tried to sue Pixar-Disney for producing and selling lamps in the likeness of Luxo Jr without having obtained authorization to do so. Both parties reached an agreement: Luxo Jr would remain as the Pixar logo but they would stop selling the lamps.

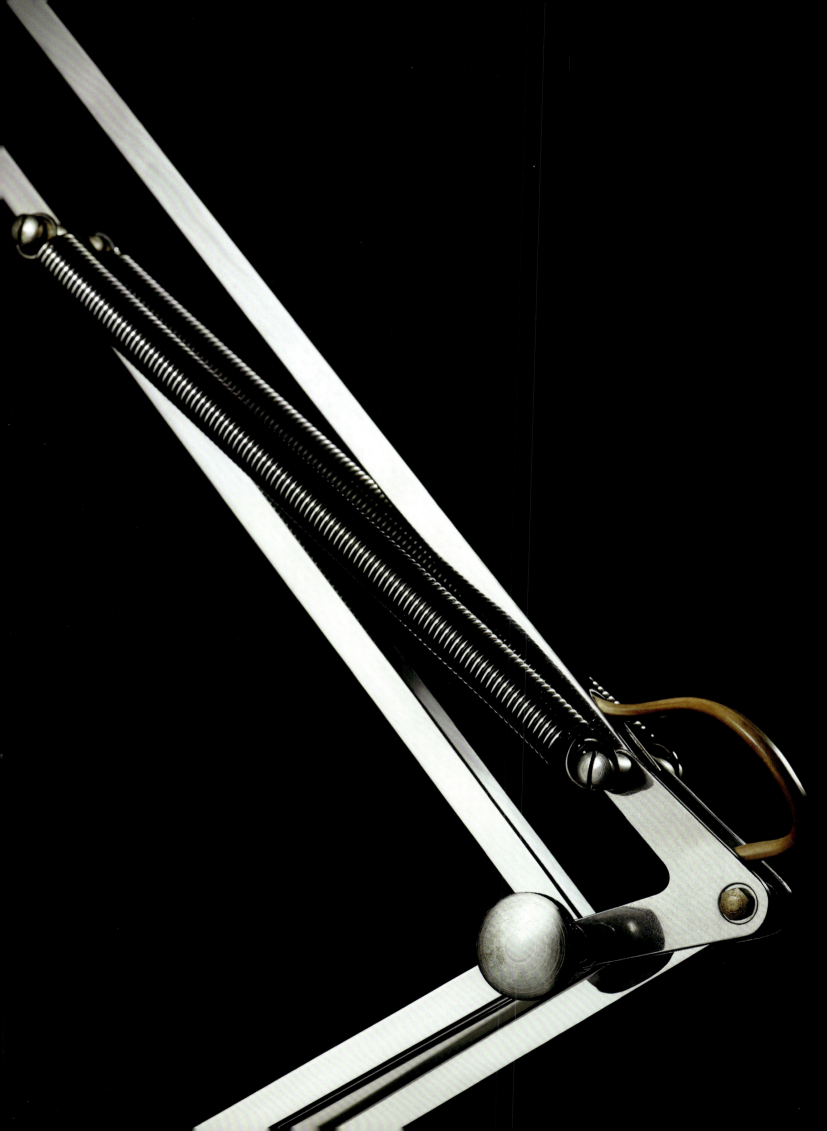

HEALTH CHAIR

THE IRONRITE IRONER CO. / 1938

It was in the city of Detroit that two partners, Herman A. Sperlich and Johannes M. Uhlig, invented the famous 'mighty Ironrite', an 'all-powerful' ironing machine, in the late 1920s. During this decade, machines intended to simplify domestic tasks had already appeared in homes across America.

The advertising claimed that the Ironrite ironing machine was 'the key to freedom and happiness', a miraculous invention that would help its users to preserve their 'looks and health' and keep 'their manicure intact'. Packed with reasons to be happy, the Ironrite was used from a seated position, enabling housewives to 'relax when tired from other chores'.

The extremely canny Sperlich and Uhlig also invented a chair that was specially designed for the well-being of their customers: in 1938 they marketed the Health Chair, which promised 'scientifically correct' posture. In order to be suitable for use with the machine, it measured 68 cm (26¾ in.) in height with the ironing seat at 45 cm (17¾ in.). The supposedly comfortable and ergonomic backrest and seat were made from

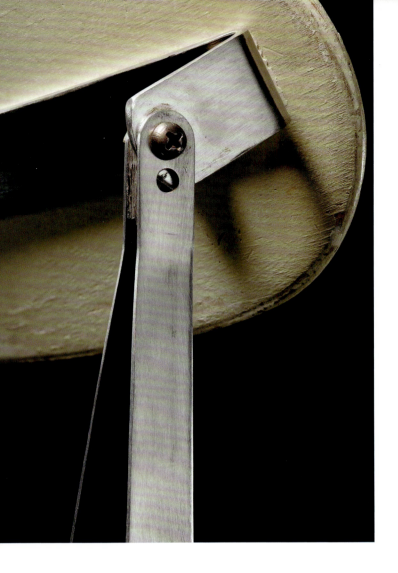

veneered wood in light colours, with an innovative steel 'suspension' base. The chair had a pure look that was deliberately in keeping with the stylistic codes of 'health' furniture.

Slowed during the Second World War, production of the Health Chair increased after 1945. Trainers and instructors criss-crossed the country to provide the free 'lessons' offered by Ironrite, either in 'ironing schools' or in housewives' homes. They never went without their Health Chair, which in this way spread throughout American homes.

Production of this chair was halted at the start of the 1960s, at the same time as the ironing machine for which it had been designed.

The mid-century modern style of the Ironrite Health Chair makes it extremely desirable among 21st-century collectors, and it officially swells the ranks of 'design icons' in the permanent collection of MoMA in New York.

LEVALLOIS LAMP

SOCIÉTÉ ANONYME R.G. / C. 1940

'Work tool' *par excellence*, this lamp was designed solely to be used by garage owners and car mechanics, and it is now possible to unearth them only through these mechanics. Extremely functional, this caster-mounted lamp allowed an engine to be lit from either above or below: mechanics could connect them to a portable lamp with which they could then focus the light on to a precise point or a tool.

This garage lamp owes its nickname to an inscription placed on its cast-iron tripod base. It includes the name of the city of Levallois followed by the initials 'RG' and the description 'Made in France'. The Société Anonyme R.G., based at 125, rue Jules-Guesde in Levallois (it moved from there in the 1970s), specialized in washing gantries, painting booths and tools for garages, as well as offering 'infrared in all its uses'.[1]

Two different models were made by the same manufacturer.[2] Dealers specializing in industrial furniture know them by the names 'Mécano' and 'Carossier'. The first (available in black, red and sky blue, and in a mounted version) was intended solely for lighting. The second model, an impressive 2.5 m (8 ft 3 in.) in height, was capable of drying the paint on car bodywork. Its broad base supported a wide aluminium shade, which gave out light from seven bulbs.

Thanks to the famous shoe designer Roger Vivier (1907–98), in the 1960s the Levallois moved from the garage to the more refined atmosphere of a bedroom

in a comfortable apartment on the Quai d'Orsay in Paris. Fond of 'mixing styles'[3] and loyal to his belief that 'everything that is beautiful can live side-by-side', Vivier used this lamp to light the objects in his collection, displayed on the shelves of an alcove.[4]

The Levallois has since inspired the creation of other designs, such as the polished steel HOK standard lamp fitted with a neoprene lampshade, designed by Christophe Delcourt. In 2008 it was reissued by the firm Coudanne & Cie, under the name of Lamp 'O'.

1 A technique used in the automobile industry for making paint dry. This information is taken from a 1967 letter addressed to the mayor of Levallois, one of the few documents providing information about the company (with the company registry number 'Seine 57 B2644').
2 'Industrial' antiquarians have now identified three garage lamps: the Levallois, the Desvil and a third model that has yet to be attributed to a particular manufacturer.
3 http://www.paris-lifestyle.fr/paris-tendances/paris-coulisses/bruno-frisoni-reinvente-roger-vivier
4 Photograph published in Thomas Kernan (ed.), *Nouvelles réussites de la décoration française: 1960–1966*, Paris, 1966.

Several elements allow the birth of the Levallois lamp to be dated to the 1940s: the presence of cast-iron knobs, the moulded signature on the base, and the fabric-covered cable.

ENVOY LINE SCHOOL DESK

AMERICAN SEATING / 1941

The recent vogue for vintage furniture has brought this chair back into the public eye. Beautiful, cleverly designed and with a timeless charm, the Envoy Line school desk goes straight to the top of the class.

The American Seating Company celebrated its 125th anniversary in 2011. The millions of seats sold by AS have equipped amphitheatres, cafeterias, auditoriums, public places (including New York's Madison Square Garden) and classrooms. Schools were the first to take advantage of the furniture produced by this firm, founded in 1886 in Michigan under the name Grand Rapids School

Furniture. It quickly became a force to be reckoned with on the international market for school furniture, which it still dominates today.

The Envoy Line series was designed in 1941 and based on a technological innovation that was unprecedented in this field: one-piece steel construction. The base, sides and back upright are in fact one single piece; the wooden backrest and seat are then added afterwards. The lower bar of the backrest swivels to accommodate the angle of a child's back. This lightweight piece of furniture is available in four sizes,

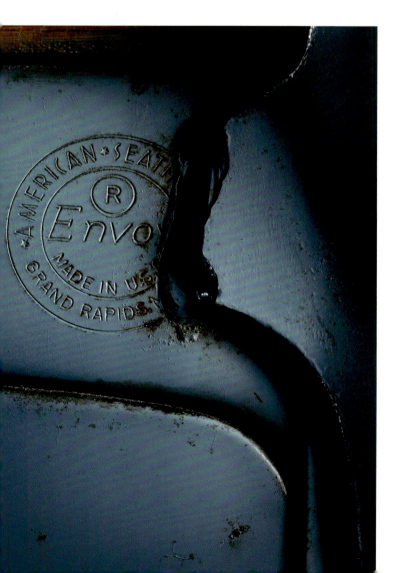

The streamlined appearance,
lightness and clever design of
the Envoy Line school desk from
American Seating make it a
timeless classic.

ranging from 28 cm (11 in.) to 45 cm (17¾ in.) in height for the chair, and three sizes for the version including a small desk top, from 33 cm (13 in.) in height upwards, with open or enclosed casing. Adjustable in height, the desk version also includes a bookshelf under the seat. Not only ergonomic, it also had an educational impact: the double-seat desks and then separate tables and chairs that would later predominate were still far away.

What makes the Envoy Line desk successful, in the past as well as now, is its famous streamlined style that was so dear to designers of the 1930s and 1940s: a pared-down, aerodynamic profile often associated with boats, cars and aeroplanes.

At the 'Design for Kids' auction held by Pierre Bergé and Associates in Brussels in December 2010, an Envoy Line desk in plywood and light-brown painted steel from 1941 was sold for €250.

NAVY CHAIR

EMECO / 1944

Emeco's Navy Chair has spent a long time sailing the seven seas. A privilege reserved for icons of design, it now makes cameo appearances in television series or is made over by famous designers. The secret of its longevity is in its composition and, perhaps, in the neutrality of its lines, something described by Philippe Starck as a certain 'absence of style'.[1]

Four hours and a series of fifty different actions are required to complete the 77-step process by which a Navy Chair is created.

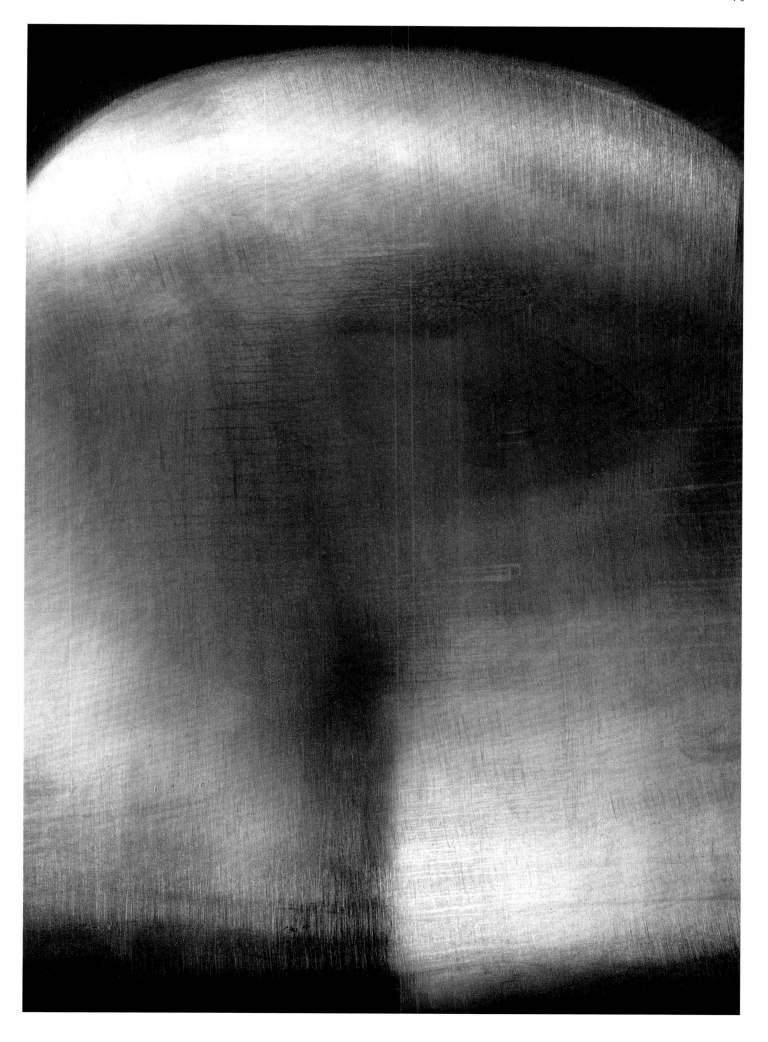

In the mid-20th century, aluminium became a force to be reckoned with in the manufacture of industrial furniture. The use of this extremely malleable metal grew considerably during the war; it is present in large quantities in nature and since the start of the last century we have also begun to recycle it.[2]

In 1944, the American company Emeco, based in Pennsylvania, developed a chair consisting of 80 per cent recycled aluminium; it was named the Navy 1006, shortened to 'Ten-O-Six' in company jargon. Destined for the submarines and ships of the American military fleet, it is ultralight (3.2 kg [7 lb] in weight, 86 cm [33⅞ in.] high and 50 cm [19⅝ in.] deep), it is rustproof, resistant to breakages and anti-magnetic, this last being one of the properties of aluminium that made it highly desirable in this context.

The Cold War saw an end to its production during the 1970s. Acquired in 1998 by Gregg Buchbinder, who enlisted the services of Philippe Starck, the Emeco Company took a new direction and began to target the design community. Mission accomplished: sales jumped by 300 per cent and production tripled. Since then, Norman Foster (in 2006), Frank Gehry (2004) and Andrée Putman (2009) have all produced their own interpretations of the Navy Chair.

A sign of the times, the Emeco and Coca-Cola companies recently joined forces to create the 111 Navy Chair, a replica of the 1006, now manufactured from 111 plastic bottles of the famous drink. Its manufacture, along with its distribution by the Conran Shop in particular, allows more than three million bottles per year to be recycled.

1 Brigitte Durieux, *Le Mobilier industriel*.
2 This practice has become the norm, and it is currently estimated that more than 70 per cent of aluminium is recycled.

BLOCMÉTAL CHAIR

RENÉ MALAVAL / 1945

In post-war France, a craftsman came up with the idea of recovering munitions factory waste, specifically the long strips of metal in which bullet caps were produced. From 1945 René Malaval, a professional welder,[1] used this scrap to manufacture urban outdoor furniture. Welded and passed through a rolling device that he had developed, the strips were then hit into shape with a mallet and placed on wrought-iron U-shaped bases; in this way René Malaval's bench was born. Some of the earliest examples were purchased by the Grotto of Lourdes in 1953, and are still in use.

Chairs and tables were sold to local cafés and restaurants. The traditional manufacturing process made each piece of furniture unique, a feature that now makes them particularly popular with collectors.

On the death of René Malaval in 1957, his son Gilbert took over the company during France's thirty years of post-war economic growth. Costs and logistics were optimized through the 'simplification' of the designs and the diversification of production. Private customers fell in love with stylized garden furniture and small pedestal tables, such as the Rigitulle range by Mathieu Margot.

The same year Blocmétal won a tender with the city of Marseille to manufacture hundreds of public waste bins. These punched green bins soon spread across the whole of France. The Malaval family also designed other products intended for mass distribution, as well as a children's line that is now highly sought-after.

A new factory was set up in the Lourdes suburbs in 1968. The manufacturing process was entirely overhauled; bullet caps were now made from plastic, so Gilbert Malaval was obliged to purchase sheet metal and have it punched himself.

1 Originally from Albi and a journeyman member of the historic French artisan organization known as the 'Compagnons du Tour de France', René Malaval also took part in the construction of the first pipeline between Algeria and France.

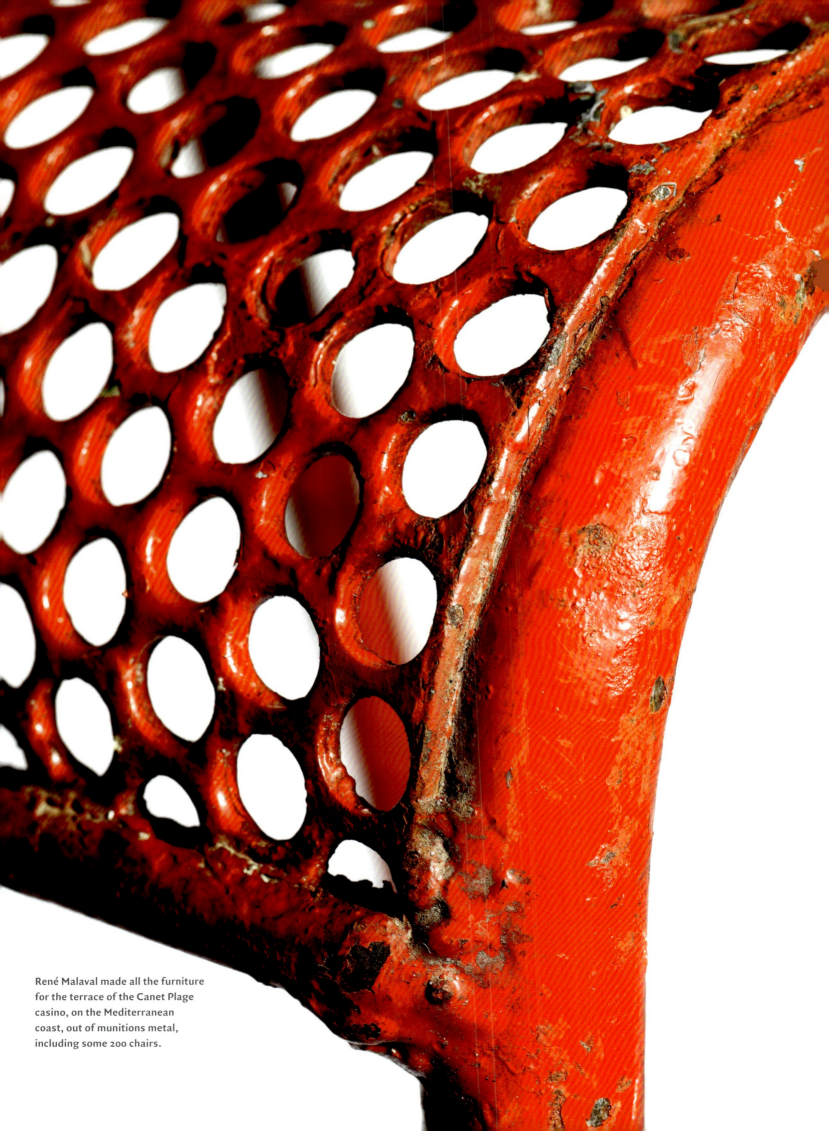

René Malaval made all the furniture
for the terrace of the Canet Plage
casino, on the Mediterranean
coast, out of munitions metal,
including some 200 chairs.

MULLCA 510 CHAIR

GASTON CAVAILLON / 1947

A chair designed between the wars, and on which millions of school children sat for many decades, discovered a vocation on the picket line in 1968. It then fell from favour before being reborn in a more modern guise, upholstered in leather.

Gustave Cavaillon, commercial director of the Parisian Furnishing Company (one of the manufacturers that supplied furniture to the state), formed the Mullca company in 1947.[1] France was then right in the middle of its reconstruction phase; it needed to produce quickly and in large quantities. Innovative, unbreakable, light and stackable, this chair offered two original features: the curve of its legs was perfectly calculated so that the backrest could not touch the walls of a classroom, and the hollow of the seat forced schoolchildren, so it is said, to sit upright. Over the years Gustave Cavaillon filed many patents in order to improve this small seat.

The chair was officially selected to be supplied to every school in France; millions were produced. In spite of itself the 510 was mixed up in the events that shook France in 1968; it was immortalized in the magazine *Paris Match*, with the employees of Sud-Aviation, the first factory to down tools and close its doors.[2] The protesting students even went so far as to use it as a projectile.

In 1985 Terence Conran brought it to Habitat, in a very chic glossy black. Having left the classroom, it would come back under the spotlight in 2007, when a Parisian design and architecture studio, Ciguë, came up with the idea of reviving the little Mullca 510 chair and re-covering it with leather. Lafa began to manufacture it again at Aurillac. Sweet revenge for a chair that the Member of Parliament Claudius-Petit had described in front of the National Assembly, at its creation, as the 'ugliest chair in the world'.[3]

1 In partnership with a Mr Müller, whom he bought out shortly afterwards: 'Mullca' took the first syllable of the name of both of its founders.
2 *Paris Match* no. 999, 29 June 1968.
3 Corinne Delvaux in *Karambolage*, on Arte, programme dated 2 September 2007.

Made of chrome and copper, the tubing can display a whole range of tones to match the colours of the leather selected.

The embodiment of nostalgic chic, the reissued Ciguë version of the Mullca 510 loves the limelight and is a real object of desire for design-lovers.

ESAVIAN LIMITED DESK AND CHAIR

JAMES LEONARD / 1948

As a consequence of the Second World War, many industries benefited from technical advances developed in the aviation industry, making extensive use of aluminium. Material shortages contributed to popularizing this metal that was both cheap and easy to find.

Formed in 1883, Esavian Limited was the brand under which the ESA (Educational Supply Association), the British leader in the school furniture market, sold its products, including books, furniture, windows and other items. From 1917 it manufactured wooden sliding doors; in the interwar period, this material was replaced with metal, and aluminium stepped into the spotlight.

Was the designer James W. Leonard one of those working for Esavian? Undoubtedly yes.[1] The desk and chair attributed to him appeared in early 1948 in the magazine *Domus*. A high-pressure machine from the United States was used to make their cast-aluminium bases.[2] Various designs for these pieces existed; they all feature a base similar to the 'compass base' that would be developed two or three years later by Jean Prouvé. Esavian sold several versions of this small desk, measuring 73 cm (28¾ in.) high, 40 cm (15¾ in.) wide and 50 cm (19⅝ in.) deep, with either one or two seats and a choice of a simple table top or a box top. The chair was made from plywood, with a padded seat and backrest covered with Formica (often yellow) or vinyl.

More than a million Leonard chairs were sold by Esavian before 1965. Perhaps too reminiscent of the difficult post-war years, this furniture eventually fell into disuse with the advent of plastic; it has now been given a new lease of life by collectors.

---

1 In 1974, the British Society of Industrial Artists and Designers announced the death of James W. Leonard, the head designer at Esavian.

2 A photograph of a classroom furnished with Leonard's chairs taken in the United States in 1949 appears in the catalogue *The Class Room, From the 19th Century until the Present Day*, by Thomas Müller and Romana Scheiner, published for 'The Classroom in the VS Museum' exhibition.

Designed for Esavian in 1948 by James Leonard, these school desks and chairs made from cast aluminium, beech plywood and pale grey vinyl were manufactured in Stevenage, Hertfordshire. These items were also widespread across the United States.

ODELBERG & OLSON CHAIR

ATTRIBUTED TO ELIAS SVEDBERG / 1948

A height-adjustable swivel chair made of wood and metal: the Odelberg & Olson is a superb example of post-war design 'in the style of Jean Prouvé'.

An inscription on the chair reads 'NORDISKA KOMPANIET Made in Sweden TRIVA'. At the turn of the century the Nordiska Kompaniet (NK), a shrine to early 20th-century trends and still one of the most design-committed department stores in Sweden, set many designers to work. Among them was Elias Svedberg, who created the Triva furniture range for the garden city of Malmö in Sweden.[1] He was a former pupil of Carl Malmsten who spent a large part of his career at NK while working abroad. Should we perhaps see a connection here with Knoll, which appears to have distributed the chair briefly in the United States?

The chair also bears the label 'manufactured by AB Odelberg & Olson', a steel-producing company that made everything from nails to pipe sections for pipelines, formed in Stockholm in 1884 by Anders Olson and John Odelberg. It is likely that the firm, like Forges de Strasbourg, wanted to draw attention to its steel production by creating metal furniture.

The uncertainty surrounding the creation of the Odelberg & Olson chair is complicated further by the existence of a similar chair with a metal and plywood structure and a steel base that was manufactured industrially, seemingly in France. An inscription on the reverse of the backrest, replicated on one of the control knobs, bears the words: 'EXPERFI – Exploitation Perfectionnements Industriels, rue Chareau Paris, licence 542 615.' Some differences can be seen in the attachment of the backrest, the lip of the seat and the adjustment knobs: a screw fitting for the Odelberg chair, Bakelite or plastic knobs for the EXPERFI chair.

Immediately after the Second World War, Elias Svedberg's furniture could be found alongside that of Alvar Aalto in the garden city of Malmö in Sweden. The subtle silhouette of his wooden chair with its steel base is at home in offices, studies and even kitchens. This chair is currently on display in galleries around the world, and its 78 cm (30¾ in.) of birch and steel are much sought-after at auctions.

1 Pierre Gencey, L'Art utile.

SANFIL LAMP

UNKNOWN DESIGNER / 1949

The Sanfil articulated lamp was depicted on the cover of the Christmas 1949 edition of the magazine *La Maison française*. Aptly, it was shown illuminating the plans for the 'ideal home' of the 1950s.

The nature of the lamp's component parts (its aluminium swivel joints in particular) allows it to be dated to the 1940s or 1950s. It was intended as much for the service sector as for industry, it illuminated machine tools and could be attached to the tables of the architects of post-war reconstruction, but we know almost nothing of the history of this hard-working lamp.[1]

In the huge gallery of the evolution of jointed working lamps, this one forms a link between Gras lamps and Jieldé lamps. The Sanfil also bridges two periods, that of the conquering of light and the mastery of its ergonomics.

Unlike the electric cable of the Gras lamp (1921), which was previously the bestseller, the Sanfil's wire runs through its steel arms and wraps around the inside of the joint, giving the lamp its name (*sans fils* means 'without wires'). In order to avoid any risk of stripping the wire when turning the lamp, and any subsequent risk of electrocution, its designer used a clever strategy: at the end of the arm a half-turn locking of the movement of the joint prevents the wire from twisting. This had the added advantage of allowing the shade to move from side to side.

The Sanfil lamp could be completely disassembled (the joints and the tubes of the arms could be separated); this was a precursor to the Jieldé lamp (1952), the arms of which were directly set into the joint.

1 We know that in 1985 it was part of the 'Lumières, je pense à vous' exhibition, on the occasion of the office lighting competition launched by the Minister of Culture, Jack Lang, in order to boost French industrial design.

The Sanfil lamp could be mounted in a clamp or on a base. Made from nickel-plated steel, the switch is located on top of the shade; the arm tubes measuring 45 cm (17¾ in.) and 30 cm (11¾ in.) are made from steel, the joints from cast aluminium and the shade from aluminium. The plate riveted on to the joint bears the inscription 'SANFIL J.L. Paris'. Both 'Citroën' grey and green versions have come to light, occasionally hammered.

STEEL CRANES

. . . .

JOUSTRA / C. 1950

. . . .

The French brand Joustra (Jouets de Strasbourg, or 'Toys of Strasbourg') was launched in 1934 by the brothers Paul and André Kosman. Their clockwork steel toys met with a certain amount of success, but it was not until after the Second World War that the Alsace firm experienced very strong growth, under the direction of Guillaume Marx. Production then diversified: electric toys, toy cars, limousines and miniature cranes propelled Joustra to the leading position in the European toy market in the 1950s. For thirty years the Strasbourg-based company was the leading producer of toy cranes, the biggest of which (no. 498) was 91 cm (35⅞ in.) tall and included a little steel driver, dressed in blue and wearing a cap.

Joustra no longer manufactures its famous cranes, but they are still collected passionately.

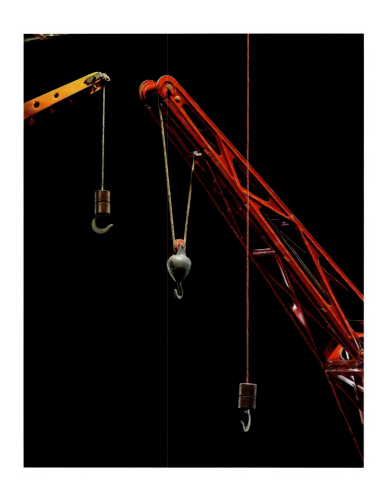

FLEXI-TUBE CHAIR

LUCIEN ILLY / C. 1950

The story of this chair reads somewhat like a novel by René Barjavel.[1] It came into being in Nyons, in the Drôme Provençale. The Flexi-tube is part of the metalworking culture of the South of France and is notable for its unprecedented technical performance.

Lucien Illy (1902–95) was a craftsman, heir to a dynasty of wheelwrights and trained in industrial drawing. He applied his knowledge to the manufacture of school furniture using wood and tubing. The chair that he created in the early 1950s was popular thanks to its flexibility, which was achieved thanks to a particular bending of the steel tubes and the wooden slats of the seat. It was Illy himself who had invented the machine for bending the tubes as well as the template for sawing the slats.

Its striking appearance made the Flexi-tube popular with hoteliers and restaurateurs, who set it up on their terraces along the Côte d'Azur, in Geneva and in Paris.

The original versions of
the Flexi-tube chair have
black steel tubing. The slats
screwed to the frame are
made from plane or beech.

Later editions of these chairs were varnished or painted blue, red, yellow or green. Others had their wooden slats replaced by metal bands or woven plastic cable.

Lucien Illy retired as the decade came to an end. He sold the patent and manufacturing licence to Établissements Eysseric, a manufacturer of machines for cutting lavender, as well as metal constructions, and stills for distilling aromatic plants sold all over the world.

Eysseric manufactured the spiral chair until the advent of the 1970s. Thanks to the use of a bending machine with roller, production then became mechanized. The manufacturer began to sell versions with seats made of metal or woven plastic, instead of plane or beech. Heavy, bulky and impossible to stack, the Flexi-tube was difficult to market, but the luxury world adopted this 'relaxation' chair, which, so it is said, began to appear in palaces from the Plaza Athénée in Paris to the Beau Rivage in Geneva.

In 2004, Christian Sapet, decorator and antiquarian at the Saint-Ouen flea market, featured it for the first time in ELLE Décoration magazine in a report entitled 'Factory Style Holds Court'.

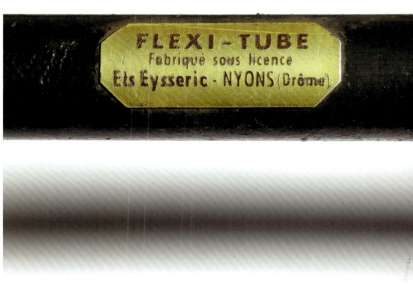

1 Lucien Illy was the son of Joseph-Casimir Illy, a wheelwright and coach builder in Nyons, who manufactured a famous 'charrette bleue', or blue cart. René Barjavel's book of the same name recounts both his youth and his life in Nyons during the period in which his mother died.

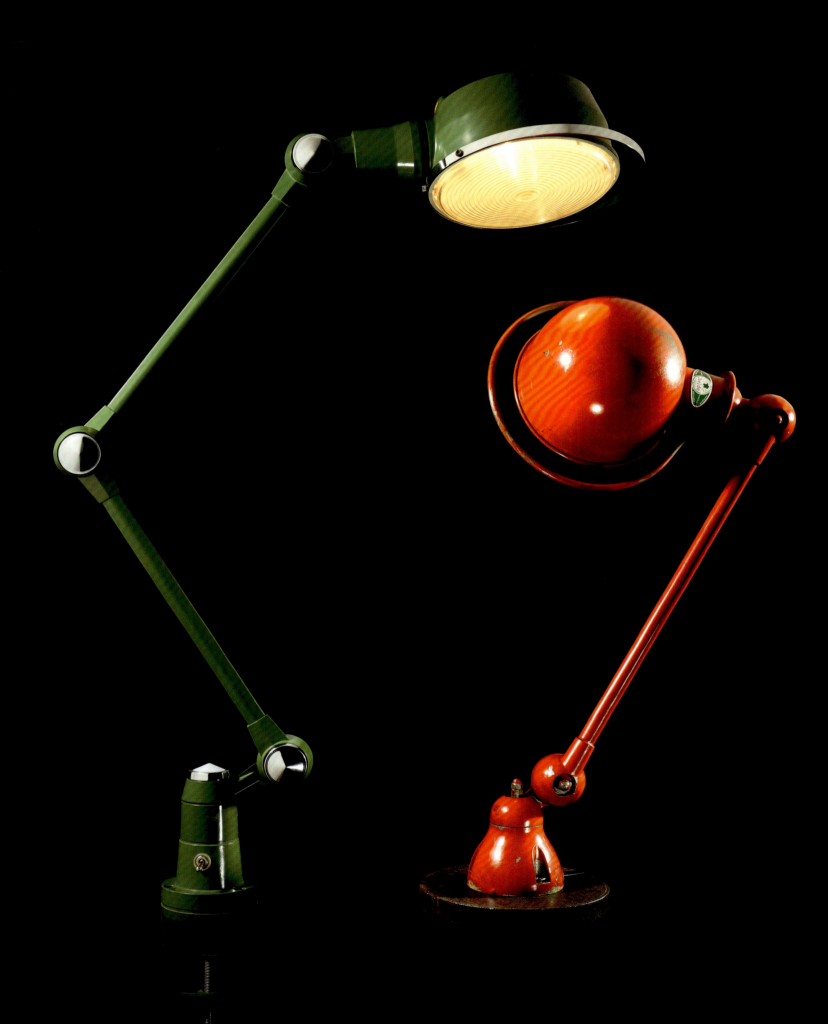

STANDARD AND LAC LAMPS

JEAN-LOUIS DOMECQ / FROM 1950

In Saint-Priest in the Rhône region of France, Jean-Louis Domecq designed the Standard in 1950 in order to optimize the lighting of his mechanics workshop; it was 'the only lamp with circular joints' according to an advertisement of the time. In fact, it functioned without any visible wires thanks to electrical contacts located within the joints. The invention became a huge success and its designer called his brand Jieldé, a name made up from his initials, J. L. D.

With its zigzag shape, spherical and adjustable head, and revolutionary ergonomics, the Jieldé Standard genuinely set a new standard for desk lamps. With two, three, four or even five arms, depending on the user's

Posing side by side: the Standard and the LAC, the two lamps designed by Jean-Louis Domecq. In the late 1960s, he completed his company's range by acquiring another Lyonnais brand, ADHER, which manufactured flexible workshop and office lamps. This strategy paid off; its expanded range allowed Jieldé to fulfil all the lighting needs of contemporary professionals.

Standard lamp: private collection. LAC lamp: François Vincent, Dijon.

requirements, it was soon found on every workbench, machine tool and architect's table. Forty years after its invention, the fact that Terence Conran chose it for the Habitat catalogue also added to its reputation; by featuring it in his catalogue he made it sacred, and the lamp spearheaded the craze for industrial style. When Philippe Bélier purchased the firm in 2002, he renamed it Loft and created the Signal lamp, a version of the Standard that was two-thirds of the original size and came in a range of different colours.

The success of the Standard led to its younger sister being almost entirely forgotten; the LAC was a covered lamp designed in 1969 and reissued in 2011. With hexagonal arms, a shade with cut-out sides and, most importantly, clever technology, it was directly inspired by the Standard. The LAC (sold from 1970 to 1990) did not achieve the levels of success expected of it, as its production costs resulted in too high a selling price. It did, however, inspire Marie-Françoise Domecq, Jean-Louis's daughter, to design the NOX, a swinging version of which only 400 were made.

With joints cast in Saint-Priest, a shade made in the Lyons area and plastic components manufactured in Oyonnax, everything in the Domecq workshop is still made in France, just as it always was.

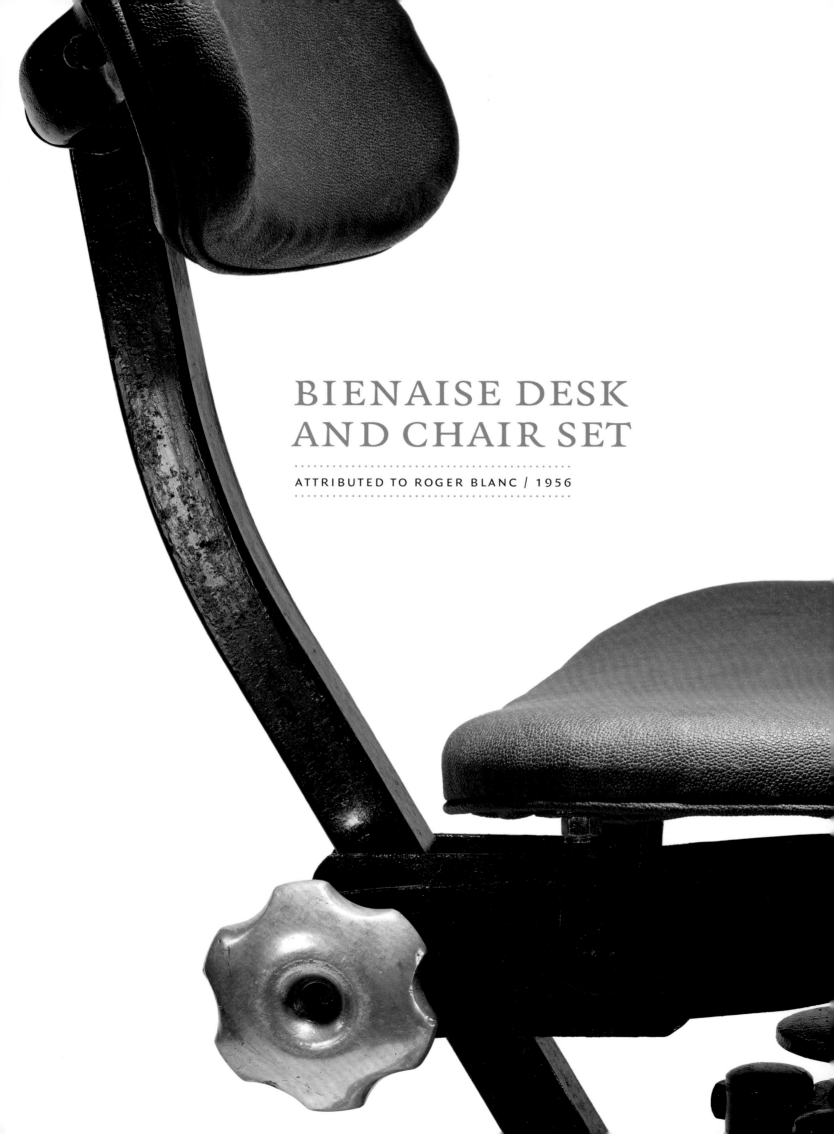

BIENAISE DESK AND CHAIR SET

ATTRIBUTED TO ROGER BLANC / 1956

A single example of this combined desk and chair set has surfaced to date. In the absence of any information about its origin, we can assume that it was produced on commission. This curious object marks a milestone in the search for comfort undertaken by Bienaise with its arched chair.

Its design is reminiscent of furniture made during the 1950s for consultation rooms in libraries or postal sorting offices and has two particular features. First, this piece of furniture is a 'one-piece' – the desk and seat are secured to a frame of bent and welded tubing. Second, the entire set is mobile, able to move backwards and forwards; on one side on a rail fixed on the ground along a wall, and on the other on two fixed casters, on the same principle as a rolling library ladder.[1]

The tubular structure of the base of the desk and the tulip base of the adjustable chair are linked to form a connected unit, 120 cm (47¼ in.) in length and mounted on casters. The seat and backrest of the chair can be adjusted by the user.

Several clues point to Établissements Bienaise as the manufacturers: the firm had already produced a chair with fixed casters that could move forwards and backwards; this chair has the same tulip base and swivelling seat. The seat can also be moved forwards or backwards like a car seat. These characteristics suggest that this item was designed to respond to the need to make space adaptable, removing fixed workstations and introducing the unprecedented notion of movement.

Roger Blanc and Paul Feuerbach, from Établissements Bienaise, stepped forward as purchasers of the firm from the Nelson Brothers in 1946.[2] Paul Feuerbach became the CEO and financial director; Roger Blanc became technical director. The latter, an engineer trained at the Arts et Métiers School, worked for a weapons design company before the war. After 1950 he launched a line of chrome tube chairs with upholstered seats and backrests with a leatherette finish (distributed to various French administrative departments), as well as factory reception chairs, stools for industrial designers and items of furniture on casters.

1 The same system is used for the Flambo typist's chair (see page 114).
2 Établissements Bienaise closed in 1961. Roger Blanc went on to invest in a furniture company in Provence.

The desk is 75 cm (30 in.) high, with a top measuring 65 cm (25⅝ in.) by 65 cm (25⅝ in.). The green moleskin seat and the green tubing, later repainted black, date this desk set to the second half of the 1950s.

FLAP DESK

JEAN PAUCHARD / 1956

Jean Pauchard formed the Tolix Company on
26 November 1954. He had solid custom from bar and
restaurant owners, for whom he supplied outdoor chairs
and tables made from sheet steel, but demand for these
products was very seasonal, leaving him in search of a
wider market. In 1958, he seized an opportunity offered
to him by the University of Dijon to furnish 200 rooms for
male students on the Montmuzard campus. He designed
and manufactured the furniture that year: a double-sided
cabinet, a desk with a tubular base and grey Formica
top, a chair, a 'UD' chair (UD stood for the University of
Dijon) made of steel tubing and leatherette, and a desk
with adjustable flap. Measuring 120 cm (47¼ in.) high
by 122 cm (48 in.) wide and 30 cm (11¾ in.) deep, the
desk stood on tubular legs and could be screwed to the
wall through two holes in its back. The materials used
in this top-of-the-range item included chrome-plated
steel, varnished plywood made from exotic woods and
grey Formica. Its manufacture reveals Tolix's high level
of expertise in bending metal, used three times in this
particular piece, and in assembling sheet metal by hand.
The small silent latch that closed the flap is a return to
the model that Tolix used for its valve-closing cabinets.

The University of Dijon called on a Parisian interior
designer to make the final colour choices for the piece. It
was, however, undoubtedly a coup to secure the services
of Steph Simon, exclusive distributor of the furniture of
Jean Prouvé, who had just installed the now famous bent-
metal posts in the Faculty of Sciences auditorium.

The flap desk and UD chair designed by Jean Pauchard in 1958. The desk, unearthed in the basement of the university residences at Montmuzard, appears in the inventory of the reconstructed room that, on the initiative of Xavier Douroux, co-director of the contemporary art centre Le Consortium, was installed in the 'Paper Log House' exhibit by the architect Shigeru Ban, shown at the Dijon Antiques Fair in May 2011.

LUMINA LAMP

MAX WILD / C. 1960

'Max Wild was a man of genius. He loved metal and understood how to transform it. His company manufactured bag clasps, and this led him to spend time in clothing workshops. This was how he came to invent a gas-powered ironing machine that made the workers' tasks easier. Then, while he was at it, he also invented a lamp that he named Lumina.'[1] Léon Glasman certainly knew his subject; he was the founder of Glasman & Compagnie, which supplied all the major textiles companies in France, including Dim in Autun and Lejaby in Yssingeaux. The Lumina lamp is now considered iconic, with its long steel legs and the curves of its shade, and can be found in the shop windows of industrial furniture dealers and at flea markets.

It was *the* lamp of the textiles industry in France during the 1960s. Set up beside the sewing machine to direct light on to the needle, it responded well to the demands of lingerie and clothing manufacturers. Consisting of more than forty different elements, which were probably outsourced to subcontractors, it was assembled on the rue du Temple in Paris, the location of Max Wild's shop, until around 1985.

In order to make it suitable for a variety of workstations and the morphology of different machines, the Lumina was available in several different designs.[2] First came the Model 23, a simple shade mounted on a rod, which, by means of a wooden screw, was fixed directly on to the machine or table; then the Model 23 20, a proper jointed lamp that was also telescopic. This lamp had a twin, the Model AB lamp, which took its name from the initials of its manufacturer, André Bordas, a sewing-machine technician who, with his sons, sold sewing machines on rue Bonnet Boulanger and made lamps from subcontracted components assembled on rue Louis-Braille.

Large numbers of these lamps ended up overseas, travelling as far as Africa and China, as a consequence of company relocations and other difficulties within the French textile industry.

1 Léon Glasman in conversation with the author.
2 Fourni Catalogue, a wholesaler of machines for the textile and clothing industry in the 1960s.

The Lumina model 23 20 consisted of one arm that was 21 cm (8¼ in.) long and another that was 27.7 cm (11 in.) long, connected with a ball joint through which the wiring ran, and a telescopic arm 24 cm (9½ in.) long, giving it an overall reach of 53 cm (20⅞ in.). This lamp was fixed by a clamp or screwed on to the working surface. Various shades made from pressed aluminium or Bakelite could be fitted to it, most of them conical in shape.

A risk of electrocution posed by wear on the wire inside the ball socket meant that the various designs included safety features: some of them were supplied with only 12 volts, and the 220-volt models were fitted with a built-in transformer from the 1970s onwards. The manufacturer's name is not always marked consistently: the words 'LUMINA SGDG' may be found on a sticker on the shade or stamped into the aluminium joint.

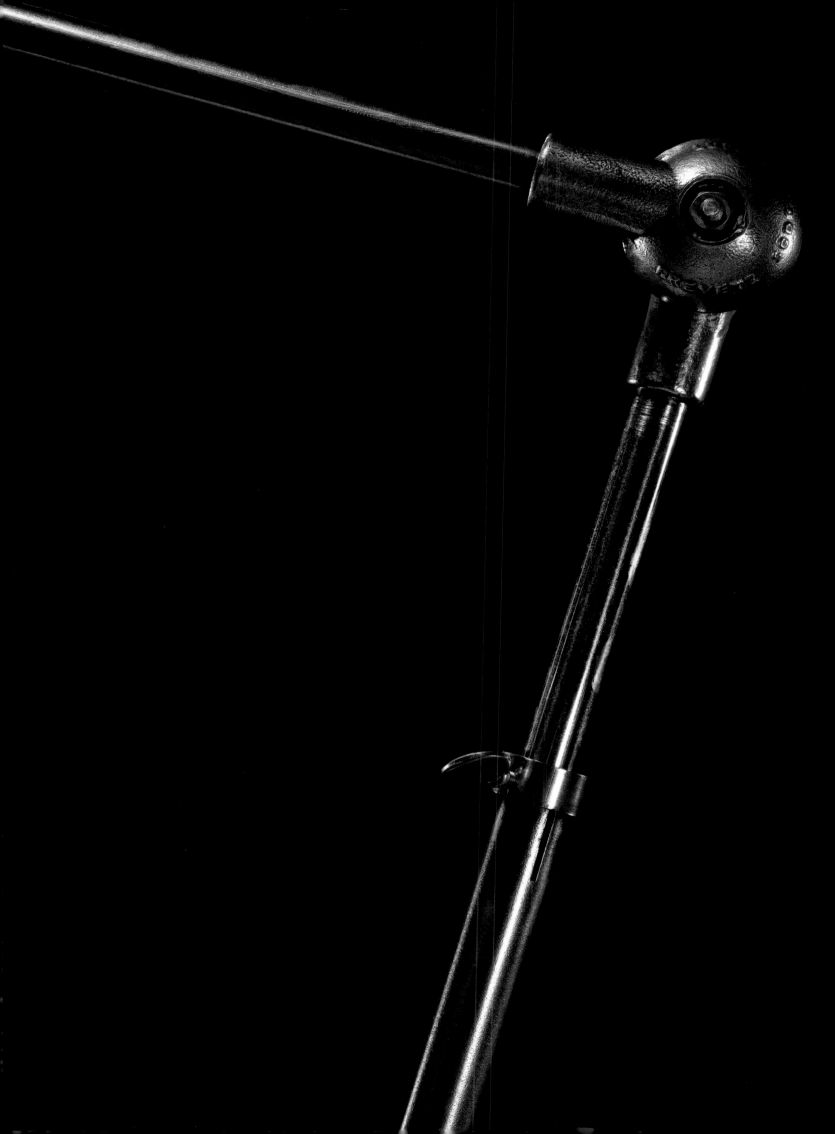

MODEL 103 FLAMEPROOF LAMP

MAPELEC / 1960

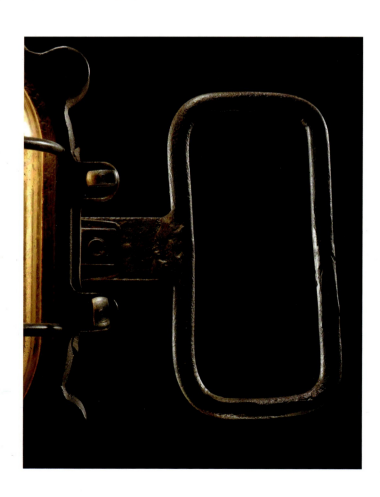

For mineworkers, the invention of the flameproof lamp[1] was a huge safety advance, greatly reducing the risk of firedamp explosions. In 1877 Jules Verne described this phenomenon in his novel *The Underground City*: 'the monk, as we called him, with his face masked, his head muffled up, all his body tightly wrapped in a thick felt cloak, crawled along the ground and with his right hand he waved above his head a blazing torch. When the firedamp had accumulated in the air, so as to form a detonating mixture, the explosion occurred without being fatal. Sometimes the "monk" was injured or killed in his work, then another took his place. This was all done in mines until the Davy lamp was universally adopted.'

During the 1950s, significant safety measures were taken by the petrochemical and chemical industries. In the second half of the decade, the French mining industry and electricity union imposed the use of standardized electrical equipment, which was required to have flameproof casing. In Amiens, the fledgling company Mapelec (Manufacture d'Appareillage Électrique) began to develop devices of this type. In 1947, the firm's founder, Henry Thickett, an engineer of British origins,[2] had built his reputation on another safety invention:

lighting boxes installed on electrical posts, offering farmers fast and reliable access to low voltage electricity.

Mapelec developed a wide range of flameproof products from the 1960s onwards, including boxes, plugs, junction boxes, switches, lamps, lanterns and floodlights.[3] These can still be found today in Paris: in the Métro, in the tunnels of the Boulevard Périphérique, outside the Louvre, and in Cannes, where they are used for deterring members of the public from sleeping on the beach.

Since those days, technology has made huge advances. Now it is the components, and not merely the casing, that are flameproof. The Mapelec factory in Amiens now equips Total refineries and around a hundred industrial sites across France that require increased levels of safety. Who knows, perhaps these items will become the antiques of the future.

1 A device designed to operate in a flammable atmosphere, fitted with a special casing that prevented it from breaking, deteriorating or spreading fire in the event of an internal explosion.
2 His grandson Eric now runs the company, which has since become part of the US-owned Emerson group.
3 Lamps (103–105), lanterns (106, 109, 1060, 1090, 1095), floodlights (800–806).

FURNITURE FOR WORKERS' ACCOMMODATION

JEAN PAUCHARD / 1971

Jean Pauchard designed three styles of room for this project, but in the absence of a real design studio, he was not able to pursue this more creative aspect of his career. 'I therefore chose to work on public commissions for large administrations, something that guaranteed our freedom and control of our prices,' he said, shortly before he died.

In the early 1970s, the French lingerie firm Dim began its relocation to Romania. In order to accommodate Eastern European workers who had come to be trained in Autun, at the company's French headquarters, a wing was added to their hostel for young workers. The contract for furnishing these sixty-nine rooms was given to Tolix. In his designs, Jean Pauchard revisited a principle he had adopted in 1957 when furnishing rooms at the Dijon University halls of residences: a double cabinet was used to divide the room into a living area and a washing area.

In response to the financial constraints imposed by the contract, the company used square tubing that was easier to weld, as well as chipboard and laminate for the shelving unit, the top of the bedside table and the dressing table. The choice of colours, lighting and textiles, with a decidedly Pop Art feel, are evidence of Jean Pauchard's attention to decorative detail. He also incorporated a moulded white plastic chair with a tulip base, reminiscent of Saarinen's designs.

The project also gave Tolix a chance to demonstrate its expertise with perforated sheet metal, which was used for the bedside table. This skill has been demonstrated more recently by the reissue of the Dédale shelving unit by Mathieu Matégot (designed in 1956) and by perforated metal versions of the Model A and A56 chairs.

In 2007, thirty-five years after it was designed, the furniture in these rooms was dispersed as part of major renovation works. It represents one of the rare attempts to produce communal furniture that was both inventive and rational.

SHOPS, MAKERS, MARKETS AND GALLERIES

UK

Alfies Antique Market
13–25 Church Street
Marylebone
London NW8 8DT
www.alfiesantiques.com

Brick Lane Market
Brick Lane
Shoreditch
London E1 6PU
www.visitbricklane.org

LASSCO Brunswick House
30 Wandsworth Road
Vauxhall
London SW8 2LG
brunswick@lassco.co.uk
www.lassco.co.uk

LASSCO Three Pigeons
London Road
Milton Common
Oxfordshire OX9 2JN
3pigeons@lassco.co.uk
www.lassco.co.uk

The Old Cinema
160 Chiswick High Road
London W4 1PR
www.theoldcinema.co.uk

Old Spitalfields Market
16 Horner Square
Spitalfields
London E1 6EW
info@oldspitalfieldsmarket.com
www.oldspitalfieldsmarket.com

Portobello Market
Portobello Road
London W10 5TD
www.portobelloroad.co.uk

Quirky Interiors
Workshop in Harpenden, Hertfordshire;
visit by appointment
james@quirkyinteriors.co.uk
www.quirkyinteriors.co.uk

Trainspotters
Unit 1, The Warehouse
Libby's Drive, Stroud
Gloucestershire GL5 1RN
info@trainspotters.co.uk
www.trainspotters.co.uk

Vintage Industrial Furniture
Workshop in Ashbourne, Derbyshire;
visit by appointment
ken.wilkinson@w3z.co.uk
www.vintageindustrialmetal.co.uk

UK ONLINE

Alexander & Pearl
mail@alexanderandpearl.co.uk
www.alexanderandpearl.co.uk

Bubbledrum
info@bubbledrum.co.uk
www.bubbledrum.co.uk

In the Wood Shed
inthewoodshed@me.com
www.inthewoodshed.co.uk

USA

Big Daddy's Antiques
3334 La Cienega Place
Los Angeles, CA 90016
bdantiques@gmail.com
www.bdantiques.com

Big Daddy's Antiques
1550 17th Street
San Francisco, CA 94107
sfinfo@bdantiques.com
www.bdantiques.com

Factory 20
Abingdon, VA 24210
eric@factory20.com
www.factory20.com

Hell's Kitchen Flea Market
West 39th Street & 9th Avenue
New York, NY 10018
info@hellskitchenfleamarket.com
www.hellskitchenfleamarket.com

Industry West
2604 Power Avenue, Suite 2
Jacksonville, FL 32207
info@industry-west.com
www.industry-west.com

Junk Style
Linda Bradford, CID
Belmont Shore, Long Beach, CA 90803
cr.bradford@yahoo.com

Modern 50 Artist Collective + Atelier
Paint Branch Park
Maryland, MD 20783
Dino@Modern50.com
www.Modern50.com

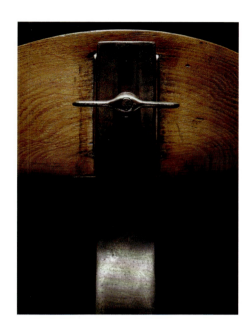

Obsolete
222 Main Street
Venice, CA 90291
what@obsoleteinc.com
www.obsoleteinc.com

Urban Archaeology
143 Franklin Street
New York, NY 10013
NYdowntown@urbanarchaeology.com
www.urbanarchaeology.com

The SHOP by H.Bleu
2124 Lincoln Boulevard
Venice, CA 90291
info@shophbleu.com
www.shophbleu.com

Three Potato Four
376 Shurs Lane, Building A
Philadelphia, PA 19128
info@threepotatofourshop.com
www.threepotatofourshop.com

Vintage Industrial
Phoenix, Arizona
greg@retro.net or scott@retro.net
www.shop.retro.net

V&M
V&M – Corporate Office
270 Lafayette Street
Suite 1400
New York, NY 10012
info@vandm.com
www.vandm.com

FURTHER READING

Audoux, Marguerite, *Marie Claire's Workshop*, translated by Frank Stewart Flint, Chapman & Hall, 1920.

Böhm, Florian, editor, *KGID (Konstantin Grcic Industrial Design)*, Phaidon Press, 2005.

Durieux, Brigitte, *Inoxydable Tolix*, Éditions de la Martinière, 2008.

Durieux, Brigitte, *Le Mobilier industriel*, Éditions de la Martinière, 2009.

Educational Supply Assn Ltd, Stevenage: Sales Catalogues *c.* 1920–60, Hertfordshire Archives.

Fiell, Charlotte and Peter, *1000 Chairs*, Taschen, 2005.

Fiell, Charlotte and Peter, *Modern Furniture Classics: Postwar to Post-Modernism*, Thames & Hudson, 2001.

Fiell, Charlotte and Peter, *Scandinavian Design*, Taschen, 2003.

Halterman, Charles (editor), *Steelcase: The First 75 Years*, Steelcase, 1987.

Hiller, Nancy R., *The Hoosier Cabinet in Kitchen History*, The Indiana University Press, 2009.

Jensen, Aage Lund, Heath, Ditto and Heath, Adrian, *300 Years of Industrial Design*, A & C Black, 2000.

Julier, Guy, *The Thames & Hudson Dictionary of Design Since 1900*, Thames & Hudson, 2004.

Kandeler-Fritsch, Martina, Hackenschmidt, Sebastian and Wagner, Monica, *Industrial Furniture: Prototypes of the Modern Era*, Verland für moderne Kunst Nürnberg, 2011.

Kron, Joan and Slesin, Suzanne, *High-Tech: The Industrial Style and Source Book for the Home*, Clarkson Potter, 1984.

Lefranc, Georges, *Histoire du travail*, Flammarion, 1957.

Les Schneider, *Le Creusot: A Family, a Company, a City (1836–1960)*, exhibition catalogue, Musée d'Orsay, 28 February–21 May 1995.

Müller, Thomas and Scheiner, Romana, *The Classroom: From the Late 19th Century Until the Present Day*, Ernst Wasmuth Verlag, 2010.

Ouvrage Collectif, *New Home Furniture Design (Industrial Design)*, Instituto Monda de Ediciones, 2007.

Raisman, David, *History of Modern Design* (2nd Edition), Laurence King Publishers, 2010.

Saint-Loup, *Renault*, Bodley Head, 1957.

Teissonière, Didier, *La Lampe Gras*, Norma Éditions, 2008.

Vailland, Roger, *325,000 Francs*, Hodder Arnold H&S, 1975.

Vellay, Dominique, *La Maison de Verre: Pierre Chareau's Modernist Masterwork*, Thames & Hudson, 2007.

Verne, Jules, *The Underground City*, translated by Sarah Crozier, Luath Press, 2005.

Verne, Jules, *The Begum's Millions*, edited by Arthur B. Evans, translated by Stanford L. Luce, Wesleyan University Press, 2005.

Weil, Simone, *La Condition ouvrière*, Gallimard, 1951.

Online

Antique home style:
www.antiquehomestyle.com/inside/kitchen/index.htm

Hoosier cabinets:
etsyvintage.blogspot.fr/2011/11/collecting-hoosier-cabinets.html

Knoll: www.knoll.com

Rosemary Thornton, The Bungalow Craze and The Germ Theory:
www.searshomes.org/index.php/2011/02/22/the-bungalow-craze-and-the-germ-theory

ACKNOWLEDGMENTS

Brigitte Durieux

They opened their workshops to us, entrusted us with their archives and came with us on our journey of discovery. Many thanks to the 'Industrial Five', whose help and support has been so valuable to us: Gilles Oudin and Jérôme Lepert in Paris, Laurent Ardonceau and Bernard Mouiren in Isle-sur-la-Sorgue, and François Vincent in Dijon.

They are the heirs to these objects and told us their history: many thanks to Colette Malaval, Lucette Eysseric, Philippe Scherf, Christian and Jean-Louis Blanc, Claire Illy, Anja Specht and Eric Thickett.

They lent us their treasures and told us their secrets: thanks to the Maison Hermès, Manuela (Tous Sens lamp), Emmanuel Jourgeaud (Midgard lamp), Sonsofvintage (Navy chair), Balouga (Esavian desk), Isabelle Moulin (American Seating desk), Numéro 74 (Esavian chair), Jérôme Delor (inspection lamps), Mr Molina (Arras chair), Éric Emeri (kitchen cabinets) and Carole Daprey.

They manufacture or reinterpret the icons of industrial design for today's market: thanks to Chantal Andriot (Tolix), Anglepoise, Société Ciguë, Philippe Bélier (Jieldé), DCW Entreprises (Gras lamp), Mackapar (Triplex), Fontana Arte (Luxo).

They exhibit these icons to best advantage: thanks to the Villa Noailles in Hyères, and the Merci concept store in Paris.

They wrote this story with me: thanks to Dominique Balland, Evelyne Raisky, Philippe Magnen, Yannick Guillemin and Catherine Fornier.

Their books bring a passion for industrial design to the general public: thanks to Éditions de La Martinière, especially to Anne Serroy, director of La Martinière Styles, and special thanks to Isabelle Parent, the most industrious of editors.

He used his talent to turn these objects into icons: thanks to Laziz Hamani and also to Antoine Lippens, for this great partnership that was initiated by Grégoire Delziani.

Laziz Hamani

My special thanks go to Brigitte Durieux, who has been a guide and an inspiration to me, and has taken me on a journey into a new world that I love.

I would also like to thank all the shop-owners, antiques dealers and collectors who were kind enough to lend us their objects, no questions asked. It was thanks to them that I learned the history of all of these objects; their passion was infectious.

Special thanks to my assistant Antoine Lippens, whose skills allowed me to take these images. They simply couldn't have existed without him. Thanks also to 414 Pixel Mixer and their team who made the photographs look so good.

Additional thanks to everyone else who worked on this book: Romuald Habert, Pascal Gillet, Lucien Audibert, Lou Levy.

I dedicate this book to my children Yannis, Mathis and Noham, who always let me discover the world in a new way, through their innocence.

Translated from the French *Les Objets culte du mobilier industriel* by Laura Bennett

First published in the United Kingdom in 2012 by Thames & Hudson Ltd, 181A High Holborn, London WC1V 7QX

British Library Cataloguing-in-Publication Data
A catalogue record for this book is available from the British Library

ISBN: 978-0-500-51663-8

Printed and bound in Italy

To find out about all our publications, please visit **www.thamesandhudson.com**. There you can subscribe to our e-newsletter, browse or download our current catalogue, and buy any titles that are in print.